Contents

Meeting Individual Needs: Advanced Students

Houghton Mifflin Reading's materials for Reaching All Learners are a time-saving system of instruction. With this group of handbooks you can turn your attention to specific needs in your classroom—to advanced students, students who are struggling below level, or students who are learning English—while other students work independently. The Challenge, Extra Support, and English Language Learners handbooks are each tied to the core instruction in *Houghton Mifflin Reading*. For independent work, the *Classroom Management Handbook* provides meaningful activities related to literature selections and to core skills.

As a group, the handbooks for Reaching All Learners:

- help you manage your classroom and organize your time effectively

- provide excellent, additional instruction

- give you the resources you need to help all students achieve grade level expectations

Challenge Handbook Overview

The *Challenge Handbook* has been developed to help you deliver instructional activities to advanced learners that will extend their experiences with the literature and skills in *Houghton Mifflin Reading*, challenging them to use higher-level thinking in interactive and meaningful ways.

The activities are presented in a five-day plan that uses the Challenge Masters and teacher support in this handbook and that also recommends use of the provisions for Challenge students in other components of *Houghton Mifflin Reading*. Your Teacher's Edition provides Challenge suggestions at point of use and in the Theme Resources section.

Students should be challenged to engage in higher-level thinking and explorations that are integrated with the learning of the larger group.

Students Who Need a Challenge

Students for whom the Challenge Activities are intended are those who are often called gifted and talented or advanced learners. They meet one or more of these criteria:

- They have mastered the core content and are ready for a challenge; they may be English Language Learners if they have adequate proficiency English.

- They are reading and writing one or two grades above their designated grade.

- They have a record of task-commitment and independence and can work at a more advanced level.

See the *Teacher's Assessment Handbook* for recommendations for identifying students who are ready for a challenge. Group students flexibly, as the *Classroom Management Handbook* recommends, to provide a challenge to as many students as can profit by it and to encourage ideas to flow among mixed-ability groups.

Preparing Students to Work Independently

Prepare students to work independently—individually, in pairs, or in small groups. Work with students to develop guidelines for independent work. Plan with them some strategies to use if they are stuck and need help. Make sure they know where to find material resources. (See also the *Classroom Management Handbook.*)

Challenge students benefit from the interaction of working in small groups or pairs as well as from working individually. The inquiry portion of a project often involves interviewing and interaction with others. Sharing their results with the larger groups of classmates also keeps Challenge students involved with others.

Emphasize the need for students to stay committed to the task and to plan their time. If some part of the project requires using resources outside the classroom, discuss how that work can be accommodated. Some activities, both full-week projects and shorter ones, may engage a student's interest and warrant more time. Allow extensions that are profitable, but insist that students set goals and plan for an end date.

In planning with students, be realistic about opportunities for presenting their results. A Challenge Master activity may include a range of suggestions for sharing, but you may decide to limit the audience, the time, and the place.

Some students respond well to challenges mainly because of their ability to stay committed to a task.

Instruction for Challenge Students

Advanced learners need instruction or coaching to channel their talents and to focus their ideas. Often, for new tasks, they need specific information beyond the regular classroom instruction for their grade. They need guidance to extend what they can already do and to complete products of high quality. The activities in this handbook provide that, in directions and Tips for students and in the recommendations for brief coaching and instruction on the pages for you.

Plan time each week to give the preparation provided, particularly for the major project, and check in with students occasionally to provide additional coaching.

Effective Ways to Challenge Students

Accelerate students' learning and ask them to explore concepts and content in greater depth. Ask of students a higher level of thinking, encourage flexible and creative thinking, and promote problem solving. You will do this by using Activities in the Challenge Handbook, which

Many advanced learners, while talented, need coaching to stay focused.

- are integrated with the content of the literature and skills in the themes so that students can relate to material they have already encountered, explore it more deeply, and think flexibly and more broadly about it

- are interdisciplinary, often developing a relationship between theme content and other curriculum areas

- are inquiry-based in helping students learn how to learn, to do research and to summarize, synthesize, or otherwise use what they have learned in the inquiry phase of their project

- encourage wider reading, including books, articles, and Internet resources, and ask students to collect data and ideas in various ways, such as interviewing within their classroom and beyond

- engage students in the processes at the highest levels of Bloom's Taxonomy—application, analysis, synthesis, and evaluation

- ask students to recognize and solve different types of problems

- provide exercises in multiple perspectives, such as asking students to write a different version of a selection

- focus on a genre, asking students to compare selections or to write in the genre of a selection

- provide opportunities for students to challenge each other, through games, discussions, or problem-solving situations

- call upon students to apply learning strategies, to set goals, and to plan their projects

- enable students to make choices within projects

Features of the Challenge Handbook

The Walkthrough on pages vi–ix gives a visual overview. Each major selection has these features:

- A major project that students work on for the week is on the first page of both the student's and the teacher's material. Students begin by planning and brainstorming; they move on to information-gathering, drafting, or creating— doing the project; and finally they present and share it. The teacher's page suggests how to pace the activity over five days. It provides recommendations for coaching or instruction to give students, usually on the first day, and often on the third day, and ends with suggestions for helping students present and share their projects. There are suggestions for your involvement on Days 1, 3, and 5.

- There are two shorter activities on the second page, each of which can be completed in about one hour. These cover the same range of content, skills, and modes as the week-long projects, but they are less ambitious in terms of the scope and time required.

- Connecting/Comparing Literature is a suggestion to the teacher to have students compare works of the same genre and apply comprehension skills.

- Additional Activities is a list of resources available for *Houghton Mifflin Reading*. It provides a reminder of those activities that are planned as Challenges throughout the Teacher's Editions as well as listing other books and media in the program. These resources are summarized in the Assignment Planner in the *Classroom Management Handbook*. You can select those you wish to assign to Challenge students while you are working with other groups.

Blackline Masters

At the back of this handbook are

- the student Blackline Masters for the Challenge Activities, for you to duplicate for each student.

- Graphic Organizer Masters that are called for in Challenge Activities; they can be used for other activities. They include story maps, Venn diagrams, webs, and other graphics that can help students organize their thinking.

See the Walkthrough on the following pages for more information.

The Challenge activities provide structure to encourage growth: goals and tips for students, and expected outcomes to help you direct and evaluate their work.

Walkthrough

To the Teacher

This walkthrough will familiarize you with the five-day plan that is provided for Challenge students for each selection in this level of *Houghton Mifflin Reading*. Annotations in this walkthrough introduce the major parts of the activities for five days.

Day-by-Day Plan for the Major Project

On Day 1 students plan their project; they brainstorm, do research, or gather information and ideas. On Days 2–4, they continue to gather ideas, they carry out their plan, and they share the results.

Instruction or Coaching for Challenges

Instruction or coaching is provided to enable students to work effectively at a challenging level and to ensure high-quality work.

Expected Outcome

The Expected Outcome shows the quality and quantity of work expected from a Challenge student.

Sharing

Sharing, publishing, or presenting the result is the culmination of every five-day Challenge project.

Content Area; Materials

- Any content-area connection is noted.
- Materials needed, other than paper and pencil, are listed. Some activities need Graphic Organizer Masters, which are in the Blackline Masters section at the back of this handbook.

SELECTION 3:
The Lost and Found

Challenge Master CH 1–5

THEME 1 / *The Lost and Found*

Name _____

1. My Unusual Adventure

Goal: Gather ideas and write a story about an unusual adventure.

Explore for Ideas

- Look at pictures of places in encyclopedia, magazines, or books. Pick some scenes where something strange is hidden from view.
- Imagine that something strange is hidden from view.
- Choose one picture as the setting of your story.
- Write some notes about what your story might be about.

TIPS

- Write dialogue—the words that the characters say to each other. Put quotation marks (" ") around their words.
- Describe your characters. Tell what they look like, how they act, or what they're feeling and thinking.

Begin Writing

Read your notes. Organize and develop your ideas. Then write your story.

- Think about the plot, or what happens in the story. Write the events in the order in which they will happen.
- Describe the place. Think about what you see, hear, feel, smell, and taste.

Share What You Know

Decide how to share your story. You might:

- Read your story aloud to the class.
- Work with classmates to put all your stories together in one book. Place the book in your class library.

CH 1–6 Challenge Home   Grade 2 Theme 1 / Off to Adventure!

---

1. My Unusual Adventure

150 MINUTES   INDIVIDUAL

(Social Studies)

Materials: magazines, encyclopedia, books, and other sources of pictures

DAY 1

Explore for Ideas

Challenge students to use their imaginations to see the fantastic in ordinary places. Tell them to jot notes as they look at pictures. If they get stuck, remind students to ask themselves "What if?" questions.

DAY 2

Students continue to work on this project.

DAY 3

Begin Writing

Tell students that the events in their stories should follow a logical order. Have them list the events in the order they will appear in the story. You might want to have students write a draft of their stories first so they can add or remove details where necessary.

English Language Learners: Urge students not to spend time searching for the exact word as they draft their stories. They should focus on getting their ideas on paper. Explain that they can go back and choose better words as they revise.

DAY 4

Students continue to work on this project.

DAY 5

Share What You Know

Tell students to practice reading their stories aloud before their presentations. Have them think about varying their reading speed, reading more quickly when the action speeds up and more slowly when the tension builds. You might want to publish their stories on your school or class website.

 THEME 1: **Off to Adventure!**

Expected Outcome

A good story will include

✓ a clearly and logically organized plot

✓ details that help readers and listeners visualize the setting and characters

✓ realistic dialogue

Time; Grouping

- Approximate amount of time an activity takes
- Recommendations for grouping.

2. Wait Until You Hear This!
60 MINUTES INDIVIDUAL

Provide time for students to rehearse their presentations. If there is more than one presentation for each character, be sure to order the presentations to avoid having two of the same characters speak in a row.

3. There It Is! **60 MINUTES INDIVIDUAL**

- Review with students the principal parts of a friendly letter: heading, greeting, body, closing, and signature.
- Have students review the selection and identify an item that they've lost.

English Language Learners: Allow students to work with a classmate who is proficient in English.

Additional Independent Work

Connecting/Comparing Literature ⊛

Have students compare the Leveled Reader selection *The Unusual Coin* with the anthology selection *The Lost and Found,* using what they have learned about Sequence of Events. Students may discuss or write about their comparisons.

Other Activities

- Theme 1 Assignment Cards 1, 2, 3
- TE p. 114, Literature Discussion
- TE p. 121, Writing a Poem
- TE p. 121E, Challenge Word Practice

- TE pp. R13, R19, Challenge
- Education Place: www.eduplace.com More activities related to *The Lost and Found*
- Accelerated Reader®, *The Lost and Found*

> **②**
> **Expected Outcome**
> A good presentation will include
> ✔ a clear understanding of the sequence of events in the story
> ✔ effective use of words signaling time sequence
> ✔ effective use of vocal expression

> **③**
> **Expected Outcome**
> A good friendly letter will include
> ✔ an informal style
> ✔ story details that show familiarity with the story and characters
> ✔ a heading, greeting, body, closing, and signature

Challenge Master CH 1–6

THEME 1 / *The Lost and Found*

Name _____

2. Wait Until You Hear This!

Goal: Give a short oral presentation as one of the characters from *The Lost and Found.*

TIPS

Choose Mona, Wendell, or Floyd as a character you would like to role-play. Prepare a short presentation telling about one of your adventures in *The Lost and Found.* Tell about events in the order in which they happened.

- Reread *The Lost and Found* and list all the major events.
- Number the events in the order they happened.
- Use your list to organize your presentation.

- Pick the most important events.
- Use words like *first, next, a few minutes later, then,* and *at last.* They will help the audience know the order of events.
- Use as much expression in your voice as possible.

3. There It Is!

Goal: Write a personal letter to ask about something you have lost.

TIPS

Suppose that you saw something of yours in a picture in *The Lost and Found.* Write a friendly letter to one of the characters in the book asking about the item.

- Brainstorm a story of how you lost the item.
- List questions you need answered in order to find the item.

- Ask if he or she saw the item.
- Tell them how you lost it.
- Get directions for finding your way in the bin.

Grade 3 Theme 1: Off to Adventure!   Challenge Master **CH 1–6**

SELECTION 3: *The Lost and Found*   **7**

The Activities on Masters

The three numbered activities on these pages appear on two blackline masters to be used during the week. The first master has the major project for the week. The two shorter activities on the second Challenge Master can be done any time during the week.

English Language Learners

Adaptations are provided when activities need to be made more accessible to English Language Learners.

Connecting/Comparing Literature

Connecting/ Comparing Literature is a standard recommendation to have students compare works of literature, applying the comprehension skill they learn with this selection.

Other Activities

Other Activities are challenging independent work that can be found elsewhere in materials for Houghton Mifflin Reading, referenced here as a reminder to use them.

Facsimile of Challenge Master

Heading identifies the student's blackline master. A reduced facsimile is provided here. Full-size Challenge Masters are in the Blackline Masters section of this handbook.

Challenge Masters

Full-size blackline masters are in the Blackline Masters section of this handbook.

Goal

The Goal describes a student's task. Point out the Goal, and preview the students' Activity page with them.

Tips

Tips help students produce work of high quality.

Challenges

Questions or instructions lift activities to a challenging level.

Sharing

Students are usually able to choose their format for sharing.

Name _____

1. My Unusual Adventure

Goal: Gather ideas and write a story about an unusual adventure.

Explore for Ideas

- Look at pictures of places in encyclopedias, magazines, or books. Pick some favorite ones.
- Imagine that something strange is hidden from view.
- Choose one picture as the setting of your story.
- Write some notes about what your story might be about.

Begin Writing

Read your notes. Organize and develop your ideas. Then write your story.

- Think about the plot, or what happens in the story. Write the events in the order in which they will happen.
- Describe the place. Think about what you see, hear, feel, smell, and taste.

Share What You Know

Decide how to share your story. You might:

- Read your story aloud to the class.
- Work with classmates to put all your stories together in one book. Place the book in your class library.

TIPS

- Write *dialogue*—the words that the characters say to each other. Put quotation marks (" ") around their words.
- Describe your characters. Tell what they look like, how they act, or what they're feeling and thinking.

CH 1–5 Challenge Master

Grade 3 Theme 1: Off to Adventure!

Activities 2 and 3

These two shorter activities can be done
any time during the week.

THEME 1/*The Lost and Found*

Name_____

2. Wait Until You Hear This!

Goal: Give a short oral presentation
as one of the characters from
The Lost and Found.

Choose Mona, Wendell, or Floyd
as a character you would like to role-
play. Prepare a short presentation
telling about one of your adventures
in *The Lost and Found.* Tell about
events in the order in which they
happened.

TIPS

• Reread *The Lost and Found* and list all the major events.

• Number the events in the order they happened.

• Use your list to organize your presentation.

   • Pick the most important events.

   • Use words like *first, next, a few minutes later, then,* and *at last.* They will help the audience know the order of events.

   • Use as much expression in your voice as possible.

3. There It Is!

Goal: Write a personal letter to ask
about something you have lost.

TIPS

• Brainstorm a story of how you lost the item.

• List questions you need answered in order to find the item.

Suppose that you saw something
of yours in a picture in *The Lost and
Found.* Write a friendly letter to one
of the characters in the book asking about the item.

   • Ask if he or she saw the item.

   • Tell them how you lost it.

   • Get directions for finding your way in the bin.

Grade 3 Theme 1: Off to Adventure!   Challenge Master **CH 1–6**

Challenges

A skill applied is often more advanced
than expected at this grade level.

Numbering of Masters

The numbering identifies the master as
CH (Challenge Handbook) and gives the
theme number followed by the number
of the master in the sequence of
Challenge Masters for this theme.

Theme 1

Off to Adventure!

Selections

1 Cliff Hanger

2 The Ballad of Mulan

3 The Lost and Found

Activities

1

Expected Outcome

A good oral report will include

✔ a well-organized presentation

✔ specific, clearly explained details about safe rock-climbing skills

✔ graphic organizers to clarify ideas

1. How High Can You Climb?

150 MINUTES   INDIVIDUAL

(Social Studies)

*Materials: encyclopedia or other reference sources and **Graphic Organizer Master 4***

DAY 1

Gather Details

Use graphic organizer. Emphasize its value to students as a way of focusing their work. Tell students to take their time brainstorming questions. Remind students to take notes as they read. Tell them to check what they already know for accuracy.

DAY 2

Students continue to work on this project.

DAY 3

Prepare Notes About Climbing

Tell students to use note cards only as a guide while speaking. They shouldn't write their speech word-for-word on the cards, or try to put all the details on them. Provide the following guidelines:

• Write one important idea on each card.

• Write important details that are hard to remember on the cards, such as statistics or quotations.

• Number the cards in the order in which they will be used.

English Language Learners: Have students check their pronunciation of difficult words in a dictionary and practice saying the words aloud. You may want to pair them with a primary English speaker who can help them with pronunciation and word choice.

DAY 4

Students continue to work on this project.

DAY 5

Share What You Know

Explain to students that speakers are sometimes unaware of the speed or volume of their voices. Stress that the goal is to speak at an appropriate volume and at an easy, conversational pace. If possible, allow students to use an overhead projector or tape their visual aids someplace where they can be easily viewed by the whole audience.

2. Book Talk <u>60 MINUTES</u>   INDIVIDUAL   SMALL GROUP

Materials: *adventure books*

Remind students that when discussing in small groups they should

- speak slowly and clearly
- not interrupt each other
- allow everyone in the group a chance to participate

3. Dag's Story <u>60 MINUTES</u>   INDIVIDUAL

Before students write, have them focus on the part of the story that tells about the cliff. Tell them to think about

- what their own parent might think about allowing them to climb the cliff
- why a parent would decide that climbing the cliff was okay

English Language Learners: *Cliff Hanger* includes many words related to climbing. Have students review the story and list these words. They can use the list as a word source while writing.

Additional Independent Work
Connecting/Comparing Literature

Have students compare the Leveled Reader selection *Regina's Ride* with the anthology selection *Cliff Hanger,* using what they have learned about Cause and Effect. Students may discuss or write about their comparisons.

Other Activities

- Theme 1 Assignment Cards A, 1, 2, 3
- TE p. 42, Literature Discussion
- TE p. 47, Using a Map Scale
- TE p. 49E, Challenge Word Practice

- TE pp. R9, R15, Challenge
- Education Place: www.eduplace.com More activities related to *Cliff Hanger*
- Accelerated Reader®, *Cliff Hanger*

②

Expected Outcome

A good book discussion will include

✔ comparisons to books the students have already read

✔ specific details that make the book appealing

✔ an opinion of the book that includes its strengths and its weaknesses

③

Expected Outcome

A good rewrite will include

✔ the scene told from the point of view of Dag

✔ details that develop Dag's personality and support his point of view

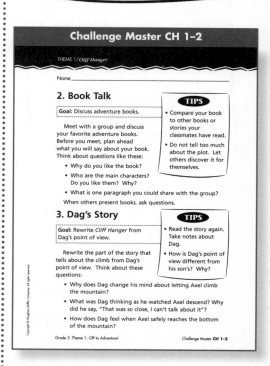

Activities

Challenge Master CH 1–3

THEME 1/*The Ballad of Mulan*

Name_____

1. *Mulan:* The Play

Goal: Rewrite the legend of Mulan as a play and perform it.

Start Gathering Details

- List the characters in *The Ballad of Mulan* and describe them. Use an inference chart like the one on page 32 of the Practice Book to help you.
- Note details about the setting.
- List each of the events in the order in which they happen.
- Take notes of dialogue and actions you want to use.

Now plan what you'll use in your play. What events will you show or tell about? How many characters will you use?

Begin Writing

Remember, you have to tell the whole story through dialogue. *Dialogue* is what actors say to each other. Write dialogue that sounds real. Sometimes you will have a change in time or place. Have your actors leave the stage briefly to mark the end of a scene.

TIPS
- Don't use too many locations for your play.
- Keep each piece of dialogue short.

Perform the Play

Present your play to your class. First give a reading of the play. Allow classmates to read the different parts. Read the play aloud, but don't act it out. Gather your actors and choose actions to go along with the dialogue. Rehearse the play the way you want it to be. Make some basic costumes from cardboard, paper, or other materials. Now perform the play.

CH 1–3 Challenge Master   Grade 3 Theme 1: Off to Adventure!

①

Expected Outcome

A good play will include

✔ a plot that tells the legend of Mulan

✔ realistic dialogue

✔ characterization that reflects familiarity with the characters' personalities

1. *Mulan:* The Play

150 MINUTES   INDIVIDUAL   SMALL GROUP

(Social Studies)

Materials: cardboard, paper, markers, glue, and scissors

DAY 1

Start Gathering Details

Have students become thoroughly familiar with the story. Emphasize that they do not have to include every event described in *The Ballad of Mulan.* They can also elaborate on events that they think are especially interesting or dramatic.

DAY 2

Students continue to work on this project.

DAY 3

Begin Writing

Check with students on their progress. Tell students that their plays will not have sets, so they must provide all the information through the dialogue, actions, and gestures of the actors. Explain that scene changes are important to help the actors and audience move from one place or time to another place or time. Refer students to "Henry & Ramona" on page 396 of *Horizons* as an example of how dialogue and action are written in plays.

English Language Learners: Tell students to draft quickly rather than pausing to find the exact word for every line. Once they have their basic ideas in place, they can revise to improve word choice and phrasing. Have them consult with more proficient English speakers to achieve realistic dialogue.

DAY 4

Students continue to work on this project.

DAY 5

Perform the Play

Provide class time for the presentations.

2. Abigail's Drum   60 MINUTES   INDIVIDUAL
(Challenge Theme Paperback)

Materials: encyclopedia, library materials, drawing paper, markers (optional), and Graphic Organizer Master 2

- Have students begin by reviewing the descriptions of Scituate Lighthouse in *Abigail's Drum.* Remind them to reread the Afterword.
- Have students use a Venn diagram to organize points of comparison for their paragraphs.

3. Dear Diary   60 MINUTES   INDIVIDUAL

- Tell students to use the skill of making inferences to learn more about Mulan.
- Have students list ideas about how Mulan might feel and things she might think about while she is gone from home.

Additional Independent Work
Connecting/Comparing Literature

Have students compare the Leveled Reader *Ida Lewis and the Lighthouse* with the anthology selection *The Ballad of Mulan,* using what they have learned about Making Inferences. Students may discuss or write about their comparisons.

Other Activities

- Challenge Theme Paperback, *Abigail's Drum*
- Theme 1 Assignment Cards 4, 5, 6, 7
- TE p. 82, Literature Discussion
- TE p. 89, Art/Language/ Writing
- TE p. 89E, Challenge Word Practice

- TE pp. R6, R11, R17, Challenge
- Education Place: www.eduplace.com More activities related to *The Ballad of Mulan*
- Accelerated Reader®, *The Ballad of Mulan*

Expected Outcome

A good paragraph will include

✔ references to Scituate Lighthouse

✔ specific details comparing Scituate Lighthouse to other lighthouses

Expected Outcome

A good diary entry will include

✔ the probable thoughts and feelings of Mulan

✔ reference to story details to support ideas and feelings expressed in the entry

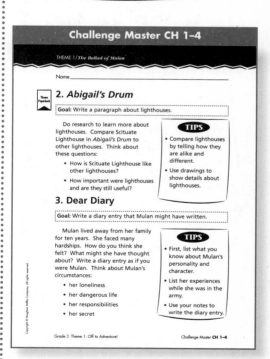

Challenge Master CH 1–5

THEME 1/*The Lost and Found*

Name _____

1. My Unusual Adventure

Goal: Gather ideas and write a story about an unusual adventure.

Explore for Ideas

- Look at pictures of places in encyclopedias, magazines, or books. Pick some favorite ones.
- Imagine that something strange is hidden from view.
- Choose one picture as the setting of your story.
- Write some notes about what your story might be about.

Begin Writing

Read your notes. Organize and develop your ideas. Then write your story.

- Think about the plot, or what happens in the story. Write the events in the order in which they will happen.
- Describe the place. Think about what you see, hear, feel, smell, and taste.

Share What You Know

Decide how to share your story. You might:

- Read your story aloud to the class.
- Work with classmates to put all your stories together in one book. Place the book in your class library.

TIPS

- Write *dialogue*—the words that the characters say to each other. Put quotation marks (" ") around their words.
- Describe your characters. Tell what they look like, how they act, or what they're feeling and thinking.

CH 1–5 Challenge Master — Grade 3 Theme 1: Off to Adventure!

---

❶ Expected Outcome

A good story will include

✔ a clearly and logically organized plot

✔ details that help readers and listeners visualize the setting and characters

✔ realistic dialogue

---

1. My Unusual Adventure

150 MINUTES   INDIVIDUAL

(Social Studies)

Materials: *magazines, encyclopedia, books, and other sources of pictures*

DAY 1

Explore for Ideas

Challenge students to use their imaginations to see the fantastic in ordinary places. Tell them to jot notes as they look at pictures. If they get stuck, remind students to ask themselves "What if?" questions.

DAY 2

Students continue to work on this project.

DAY 3

Begin Writing

Tell students that the events in their stories should follow a logical order. Have them list the events in the order they will appear in the story. You might want to have students write a draft of their stories first so they can add or remove details where necessary.

English Language Learners: Urge students not to spend time searching for the exact word as they draft their stories. They should focus on getting their ideas on paper. Explain that they can go back and choose better words as they revise.

DAY 4

Students continue to work on this project.

DAY 5

Share What You Know

Tell students to practice reading their stories aloud before their presentations. Have them think about varying their reading speed, reading more quickly when the action speeds up and more slowly when the tension builds. You might want to publish their stories on your school or class website.

2. Wait Until You Hear This!

<u>60 MINUTES</u>   INDIVIDUAL

Provide time for students to rehearse their presentations. If there is more than one presentation for each character, be sure to order the presentations to avoid having two of the same characters speak in a row.

3. There It Is!   <u>60 MINUTES</u>   INDIVIDUAL

- Review with students the principal parts of a friendly letter: heading, greeting, body, closing, and signature.
- Have students review the selection and identify an item that they've lost.

English Language Learners: Allow students to work with a classmate who is proficient in English.

Additional Independent Work
Connecting/Comparing Literature

Have students compare the Leveled Reader selection *The Unusual Coin* with the anthology selection *The Lost and Found,* using what they have learned about Sequence of Events. Students may discuss or write about their comparisons.

Other Activities

- Theme 1 Assignment Cards 1, 2, 3
- TE p. 114, Literature Discussion
- TE p. 121, Writing a Poem
- TE p. 121E, Challenge Word Practice

- TE pp. R13, R19, Challenge
- Education Place: www.eduplace.com
  More activities related to *The Lost and Found*
- Accelerated Reader®, *The Lost and Found*

---

❷

Expected Outcome

A good presentation will include

✔ a clear understanding of the sequence of events in the story

✔ effective use of words signaling time sequence

✔ effective use of vocal expression

❸

Expected Outcome

A good friendly letter will include

✔ an informal style

✔ story details that show familiarity with the story and characters

✔ a heading, greeting, body, closing, and signature

Challenge Master CH 1–6

THEME 1/*The Lost and Found*

Name_____

2. Wait Until You Hear This!

Goal: Give a short oral presentation as one of the characters from *The Lost and Found.*

Choose Mona, Wendell, or Floyd as a character you would like to role-play. Prepare a short presentation telling about one of your adventures in *The Lost and Found.* Tell about events in the order in which they happened.

- Pick the most important events.
- Use words like *first, next, a few minutes later, then,* and *at last.* They will help the audience know the order of events.
- Use as much expression in your voice as possible.

TIPS
- Reread *The Lost and Found* and list all the major events.
- Number the events in the order they happened.
- Use your list to organize your presentation.

3. There It Is!

Goal: Write a personal letter to ask about something you have lost.

Suppose that you saw something of yours in a picture in *The Lost and Found.* Write a friendly letter to one of the characters in the book asking about the item.

- Ask if he or she saw the item.
- Tell them how you lost it.
- Get directions for finding your way in the bin.

TIPS
- Brainstorm a story of how you lost the item.
- List questions you need answered in order to find the item.

Grade 3 Theme 1: Off to Adventure!   Challenge Master **CH 1–6**

Theme 2

Celebrating Traditions

Selections

1 The Keeping Quilt

2 Grandma's Records

3 The Talking Cloth

4 Dancing Rainbows

1

Expected Outcome

A good story will include

✔ a well-organized presentation

✔ a few, well-developed events that relate family traditions and values

✔ pictures that help tell the story

1. My Treasure Story 150 MINUTES INDIVIDUAL
(Social Studies)

Materials: *art paper, crayons, markers, and* **Graphic Organizer Master 1**

DAY 1

Gather Details

- Emphasize to students that their treasure need not be something that has been in the family for many generations.
- If necessary, review a cluster map. Use the graphic organizer.

DAY 2

Students continue to work on this project.

DAY 3

Write and Draw

Check with students on the progress of their stories.

- Tell students to list the events they will tell about. They should number them in the order they happened. They can use this list as a guide as they write.
- Review freewriting with students. Tell them that it can be helpful for exploring ideas and generating more details to include in their writing.

English Language Learners: Have English Language Learners write about treasures that they brought with them from their country of origin. As they write, they should explain terms, traditions, or celebrations that may not be familiar to their readers. You might wish to team them with a more proficient English-speaking student who can respond to their writing and point out unfamiliar ideas.

DAY 4

Students continue to work on this project.

DAY 5

Share Your Story

If time allows, students might choose more than one of the ideas for sharing their stories.

2. More from the Author

60 MINUTES   SMALL GROUP

Materials: *other books by Patricia Polacco*

Refer students to Houghton Mifflin's Education Place website at http://www.eduplace.com/kids to learn more about Patricia Polacco. You may wish to appoint a leader to organize the discussion group.

3. What Do You Think?   60 MINUTES   INDIVIDUAL

Tell students to first look at the pictures carefully without rereading the story. They should then go back and reread the story while looking at the pictures. Have students focus on how well the pictures tell the story.

Additional Independent Work
Connecting/Comparing Literature

Have students compare the Leveled Reader selection *Grandpa's Baseball Card* with the anthology selection *The Keeping Quilt*, using what they have learned about Author's Viewpoint. Students may discuss or write about their comparisons.

Other Activities

- Theme 2 Assignment Cards 1, 2, 3, 4
- TE p. 178, Literature Discussion
- TE p. 185, Research Skills
- TE p. 185E, Challenge Word Practice

- TE pp. R9, R17, Challenge
- Education Place: www.eduplace.com More activities related to *The Keeping Quilt*
- Accelerated Reader®, *The Keeping Quilt*

2

Expected Outcome

A good book discussion will include

✔ thoughtful contributions from each student

✔ an opinion of the books that assesses their strengths and weaknesses

✔ familiarity with Patricia Polacco's work and ideas

✔ specific comments that are well-supported with details from the books

3

Expected Outcome

A good evaluation will include

✔ an overall impression of the pictures as well as a response to individual pictures

✔ evidence to support opinions

Challenge Master CH 2–2

THEME 2/*The Keeping Quilt*

Name_____

2. More from the Author

Goal: To read and discuss other books by Patricia Polacco.

Each member of your group chooses one book by Patricia Polacco and reads it. Then the group will meet and discuss the books. Before you meet, plan ahead what you'll say about your book. Think about:

- How is this book like *The Keeping Quilt*? How is it different?
- What did you like or dislike about the book?
- Do you think others should read the book? Why or why not?

TIPS
- Take turns speaking.
- Prepare notes on index cards. Use them during your discussion.
- Support your ideas with details from the book.

3. What Do You Think?

Goal: Evaluate the pictures in *The Keeping Quilt*.

Look at the pictures in *The Keeping Quilt* again. Take notes of your ideas. Think about:

- What do the pictures make you feel or think about?
- What do they add to the story?
- Do you like the pictures? Why or why not?

TIPS
- First, tell what you think about the pictures as a whole. Then tell about individual pictures.
- When you give your opinion, tell why and give examples.

Write a paragraph that gives your evaluation.

Grade 3 Theme 2: Celebrating Traditions   Challenge Master **CH 2–2**

Activities

1. My Family Tradition 150 MINUTES INDIVIDUAL
(Social Studies)
Materials: drawing paper, crayons, and markers

Challenge Master CH 2–3

THEME 2/*Grandma's Records*

Name _____

1. My Family Tradition

Goal: Write about someone who is important in your life.

Gather Details

Think of someone important to you. This person can be a relative, such as a favorite aunt, uncle, or grandparent, or just someone special to you. Describe what this person means to you, fond memories you have of him or her, and things you do together. Make notes to answer these questions:

• Why is this person important?

• What do you do together?

• Why do you enjoy being with him or her?

TIPS

• Construct an outline to help organize your thoughts.

• Make notes of special times you've shared together.

• Use drawings to show what you do together.

Write and Draw

Organize your writing. Tell why this person is special. Tell about special things you do. Tell how often you see him or her. Next, draw the two of you together.

Share Your Story

Decide how to share your writing. You could:

• Tell your classmates about this person. Show them the picture and explain what you do together.

• Tell how long you've known this person and different things you've learned from him or her.

• Make a copy of your writing. Put it in the class library.

CH 2–3 Challenge Master   Grade 3 Theme 2: Celebrating Traditions

---

Expected Outcome

A good description will include

✔ a well-organized presentation

✔ a statement about the importance of this person in the student's life

✔ a description of activities shared by the student and this person

✔ pictures that help tell the story

DAY 1

Gather Details

Ask students to think about a family member they know well, such as a favorite aunt, uncle, or grandparent. Students might describe fond memories or shared activities. They may also think of someone else special to them who is not a relative. Tell students to focus on the following as they gather details:

• The role this relative or friend plays in the student's life.

• Why the student enjoys being with this person.

• How often the two spend time together.

• A favorite activity the two share.

DAY 2

Students continue to work on this project.

DAY 3

Write and Draw

Check with students on their progress.

• Tell students to organize their notes before they begin writing and to follow the order listed on their activity page.

• Have students identify passages or procedures that can be clarified by drawing a picture.

English Language Learners: It may be difficult to translate some terms for traditional skills. Have students use a thesaurus and dictionary and to check with classmates in order to find the necessary vocabulary.

DAY 4

Students continue to work on this project.

DAY 5

Share Your Story

Have students choose one or more of the ideas for sharing their stories.

2. *The Eyes of the Weaver*

60 MINUTES   SMALL GROUP

(Challenge Theme Paperback)

Materials: The Eyes of the Weaver *and Graphic Organizer Master 5*

Students need to read *The Eyes of the Weaver* prior to the activity. You may wish to appoint a leader to organize the discussion group. Instruct the leader to give everyone an opportunity to speak.

3. How Does It Compare?   60 MINUTES   INDIVIDUAL

Materials: Graphic Organizer Master 7

You may wish to allow students to select another book about family traditions. Review a comparison/contrast chart. Explain that the headings on the chart should be categories of ideas.

Additional Independent Work

Connecting/Comparing Literature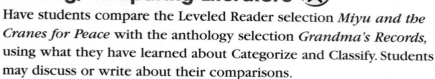

Have students compare the Leveled Reader selection *Miyu and the Cranes for Peace* with the anthology selection *Grandma's Records,* using what they have learned about Categorize and Classify. Students may discuss or write about their comparisons.

Other Activities

- Challenge Theme Paperback, *The Eyes of the Weaver*
- Theme 2 Assignment Cards 5, 6
- TE p. 206, Literature Discussion
- TE p. 213, Traditional Clothing
- TE p. 213E, Challenge Word Practice

- TE pp. R6, R11, R17, R19, Challenge
- Education Place: www.eduplace.com More activities related to *Grandma's Records*
- Accelerated Reader®, *Grandma's Records*

Expected Outcome

A good book discussion will include

✔ use of the information in the main idea chart to support ideas

✔ thoughtful contributions from each student

✔ specific comments that are well-supported with details from the selection

Expected Outcome

A good comparison will include

✔ a clear organization that shows how the books are alike and different

✔ examples and details from the books to support their comparisons

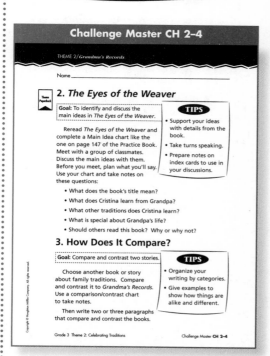

Challenge Master CH 2–4

THEME 2/*Grandma's Records*

Name _____

2. *The Eyes of the Weaver*

Goal: To identify and discuss the main ideas in *The Eyes of the Weaver.*

TIPS
- Support your ideas with details from the book.
- Take turns speaking.
- Prepare notes on index cards to use in your discussions.

Reread *The Eyes of the Weaver* and complete a Main Idea chart like the one on page 147 of the Practice Book. Meet with a group of classmates. Discuss the main ideas with them. Before you meet, plan what you'll say. Use your chart and take notes on these questions:

- What does the book's title mean?
- What does Cristina learn from Grandpa?
- What other traditions does Cristina learn?
- What is special about Grandpa's life?
- Should others read this book? Why or why not?

3. How Does It Compare?

Goal: Compare and contrast two stories.

TIPS
- Organize your writing by categories.
- Give examples to show how things are alike and different.

Choose another book or story about family traditions. Compare and contrast it to *Grandma's Records.* Use a comparison/contrast chart to take notes.

Then write two or three paragraphs that compare and contrast the books.

Grade 3 Theme 2: Celebrating Traditions

Challenge Master **CH 2–4**

Challenge Master CH 2–5

Name_____

1. The Adinkra Cloth Says . . .

Goal: Create your own version of an adinkra cloth and then write about it.

Your Own Symbols

Reread pages 224–226 of *The Talking Cloth*. Then decide what you want to say in your cloth using symbols and colors. The symbols you choose should be meaningful to you. Think about

- what you like to do
- your goals
- your personality
- your family

TIPS

- Plan what symbols and colors you will use in your drawing.
- In your chart, write in complete sentences and give details to make your explanation clear.

Draw and Write

Plan your adinkra cloth. Draw each symbol in a pattern on a long piece of paper. Next, write about your adinkra. Make a chart that tells what each symbol and color means to you. In your chart, draw a picture of each symbol. Explain what each symbol and color means. Tell why they are important to you.

Share Your Adinkra

Decide how you want to share your adinkra and your writing. You could:

- Display your adinkra. Point out the symbols and colors you used and tell what they mean.
- Place your chart and your adinkra on the bulletin board.

CH 2–5 Challenge Master   Grade 3 Theme 2: Celebrating Traditions

❶ Expected Outcome

A good adinkra will include

✔ a drawing with distinct patterns

✔ a chart with exact words and details

✔ details that give readers an understanding of the subject

1. The Adinkra Cloth Says . . .

I 50 MINUTES   INDIVIDUAL

(Social Studies)

Materials: butcher paper and markers

DAY 1

Your Own Symbols

Tell students that they can create original symbols or they can give commonly used symbols their own personal meanings. Refer them to the selection for some definitions of symbols.

DAY 2

Students continue to work on this project.

DAY 3

Draw and Write

Check with students on their progress. Tell students to plan the pattern for their adinkra. They can experiment by trying out different patterns on a small piece of paper before transferring their final pattern to the butcher paper.

Then tell students to organize their charts in a logical manner. They might follow this pattern:

- Explain each symbol and its meaning.
- Explain the significance of each color.

DAY 4

Students continue to work on this project.

DAY 5

Share Your Adinkra

Have students present their adinkras to the class in the format they chose.

2. Who Are the Ashanti? <u>60 MINUTES</u> INDIVIDUAL
(Social Studies)
Materials: encyclopedia and markers (optional)

Explain to students that their questions will help them look for the exact information they want. Review the skill of taking notes with students. Tell them to write one main idea as the heading of each card. They can then list details under the heading. Before they begin to write their report, tell students to spread the cards out on a table and place them in a logical order. Then they should number the cards and use them as a guide while writing.

3. An Inch at a Time <u>60 MINUTES</u> INDIVIDUAL

Ask students to choose a time when they learned something that was both unexpected and significant. It could be something that happened at school, but should not be assigned classwork. Tell students to describe the time, place, and people involved using vivid details. You might suggest that students use a web or list to generate sensory details.

Additional Independent Work
Connecting/Comparing Literature

Have students compare the Leveled Reader selection *Fly-Fishing with Grandpa* with the anthology selection *The Talking Cloth*, using what they have learned about Noting Details. Students may discuss or write about their comparisons.

Other Activities

- Theme 2 Assignment Cards 7, 8, 9
- TE p. 228, Literature Discussion
- TE p. 233E, Challenge Word Practice
- TE pp. R13, R21, Challenge

- Education Place: www.eduplace.com More activities related to *The Talking Cloth*
- Accelerated Reader®, *The Talking Cloth*

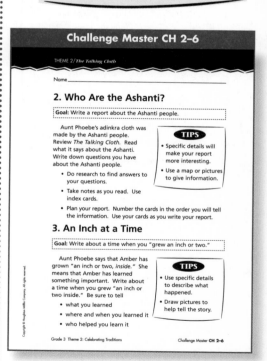

2

Expected Outcome

An outstanding report will include

✔ careful organization of information

✔ facts, not opinions

✔ details that provide information on the Ashanti people

✔ maps or pictures that show where the Ashanti live

3

Expected Outcome

An outstanding description will include

✔ examples and sensory details that bring the description to life

✔ a clear explanation of what the writer learned

Activities

1. Cultural Traditions   150 MINUTES   INDIVIDUAL
(Social Studies)

Materials: *encyclopedia, index cards, poster board, crayons, and markers*

Challenge Master CH 2–7

Name_____

1. Cultural Traditions

Goal: Find out about a cultural tradition, craft, or art and present it to the class.

Gather Information

Choose a culture that interests you. Research that culture in an encyclopedia and other sources to find out about the traditions, crafts, and arts of that culture. Pick one that interests you. Take notes about

- how it started
- why it is made or celebrated
- who teaches or makes it
- any other important facts

TIPS
- Organize your main ideas before you begin. Number your note cards.
- Follow the cards as you plan your presentation.

Write It Down

Read through your notes. Decide what your main ideas are. Write each one at the top of an index card. Then write the supporting details for each main idea on each card.

Share Your Research

Use your notes to present your subject. Some ideas:
- If your subject is a craft or art, teach the class how to do or make it.
- Give an oral presentation to your class. Use visual aids such as posters, photographs, and hand-outs to help you.
- If your subject is a tradition, act it out for the class.
- Write a report and present it to the class.

CH 2-7 Challenge Master   Grade 3 Theme 2: Celebrating Traditions

---

Expected Outcome

Good research will include

✔ well-organized information

✔ details that directly support the main ideas

✔ a creative presentation

DAY 1

Gather Information

Brainstorm with students a list of cultures they could choose from. Tell students that when they look up a culture in an encyclopedia they should be able to find a section on traditions, crafts, and arts.

English Language Learners: Have students choose a culture that is different from their primary culture.

DAY 2

Students continue to work on this project.

DAY 3

Write It Down

Check with students on their progress. As they prepare to write, tell them to organize their writing by placing the index cards with their main ideas in a logical order. Remind them to only choose details that support the main idea.

DAY 4

Students continue to work on this project.

DAY 5

Share Your Research

Have students choose a presentation format that will clearly showcase all that they have learned.

2. Who Are the Pueblo? 60 MINUTES INDIVIDUAL
(Social Studies)
Materials: encyclopedia, drawing paper, crayons, and markers

Review topic, main idea, and supporting details with students. Tell them that they should use the questions to organize their research and their writing. Stress that students should have several main ideas that are supported by details. Tell them that the answers to the questions from the Pupil's Edition could be main ideas.

3. Tell a Friend 60 MINUTES INDIVIDUAL

Remind students that they can use details from both the text and the photographs to bring the account of their visit "alive." Tell them that everything they write should be on information from the selection. However, they should use any prior knowledge and experience to help explain the events from the story. If necessary, review the five parts of a letter: heading, greeting, body, closing, and signature.

Additional Independent Work
Connecting/Comparing Literature ⭐

Have students compare the Leveled Reader selection *Drum Dancers* with the anthology selection *Dancing Rainbows,* using what they have learned about Topic, Main Idea, and Supporting Details. Students may discuss or write about their comparisons.

Other Activities

- Theme 2 Assignment Cards 10, 11
- TE p. 254, Literature Discussion
- TE p. 259E, Challenge Word Practice

- TE pp. R15, R23, Challenge
- Education Place: www.eduplace.com More activities related to *Dancing Rainbows*
- Accelerated Reader®, *Dancing Rainbows*

Expected Outcome

A good report will include

✔ a logical organization

✔ details that support each main idea

✔ map or picture that illustrates something about the Pueblo

Expected Outcome

A good letter will include

✔ many interesting details

✔ events organized in logical order

✔ proper letter format

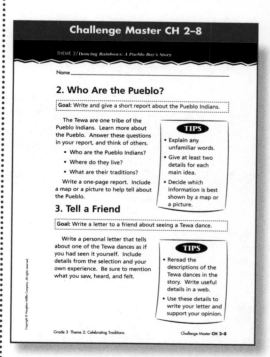

Challenge Master CH 2–8

THEME 2/*Dancing Rainbows: A Pueblo Boy's Story*

Name_____

2. Who Are the Pueblo?

Goal: Write and give a short report about the Pueblo Indians.

The Tewa are one tribe of the Pueblo Indians. Learn more about the Pueblo. Answer these questions in your report, and think of others.

- Who are the Pueblo Indians?
- Where do they live?
- What are their traditions?

Write a one-page report. Include a map or a picture to help tell about the Pueblo.

TIPS
- Explain any unfamiliar words.
- Give at least two details for each main idea.
- Decide which information is best shown by a map or a picture.

3. Tell a Friend

Goal: Write a letter to a friend about seeing a Tewa dance.

Write a personal letter that tells about one of the Tewa dances as if you had seen it yourself. Include details from the selection and your own experience. Be sure to mention what you saw, heard, and felt.

TIPS
- Reread the descriptions of the Tewa dances in the story. Write useful details in a web.
- Use these details to write your letter and support your opinion.

Grade 3 Theme 2: Celebrating Traditions   Challenge Master **CH 2–8**

Theme 3

Incredible Stories

Selections

1. Mousopolis Daily News

160 MINUTES SMALL GROUP INDIVIDUAL

(Social Studies)

Materials: *large art paper, markers, and examples of the front pages of different newspapers*

DAY 1

Gather the News

Ask students to:

- Think up *Who? What? When? Where? Why?* and *How?* questions. Then find the answers.
- Include quotations from the mice. They will have to make up these quotations, but they should use the facts from the story.
- Come up with exciting headlines to get readers' attention.
- Write an opening sentence that gets readers interested.

English Language Learners: Have students work in pairs to complete this assignment.

DAY 2

Students continue to work on this project.

DAY 3

Create the Newspaper

Meet with students and check their progress. Then emphasize to students that they should each plan their newspaper page with care so that they will have sufficient space for all the elements they want to include. They should write the headline and article first on a separate sheet of paper, leaving space for pictures and captions.

DAY 4

Students continue to work on this project.

DAY 5

Read All About It!

Provide examples of front pages of different newspapers for students to use as models.

Challenge Master CH 3–1

---

①

Expected Outcome

A good news article will include

✔ a headline that grabs attention

✔ an opening sentence that focuses on the most important idea

✔ answers to some *Who? What? When? Where? Why?* and *How?* questions

✔ direct quotations that are set off with quotation marks

2. Pupzilla 60 MINUTES SMALL GROUP

If necessary, review fantasy and realism with students. Remind them to use both elements in their sequels. Tell students to think about including dialogue. You may want to review the use of quotation marks. Tell students to be sure their sequels have a clear beginning, middle, and end. Ask volunteers to share their stories with the class.

3. Volcano! 60 MINUTES PAIR
Materials: encyclopedia and Internet access

- Students can find information at http://www.mountsthelensinstitute.org
- Have students meet to discuss the assignment, to brainstorm questions they want answered, and to divide up the research. They should meet again after completing their research to share their findings.
- Have students divide up responsibility for writing and preparing maps and diagrams.
- Provide time for students to share what they learn with the class.

Additional Independent Work
Connecting/Comparing Literature

Have students compare the Leveled Reader selection *A Town in Trouble* with the anthology selection *Dogzilla,* using what they have learned about Fantasy and Realism. Students may discuss or write about their comparisons.

Other Activities

- Theme 3 Assignment Cards 1, 2, 3
- TE p. 328, Literature Discussion
- TE p. 333E, Challenge Word Practice

- TE pp. R9, R17, Challenge
- Education Place: www.eduplace.com More activities related to *Dogzilla*
- Accelerated Reader®, *Dogzilla*

---

❷
Expected Outcome

A good story will include

✔ detailed descriptions of characters and settings

✔ events that are told in a logical order

✔ vivid dialogue

✔ an ending that wraps up the story

❸
Expected Outcome

A good research report will include

✔ a beginning that clearly states the topic

✔ a paragraph for each main idea that includes supporting details

✔ pictures, diagrams, or time lines that provide important information clearly

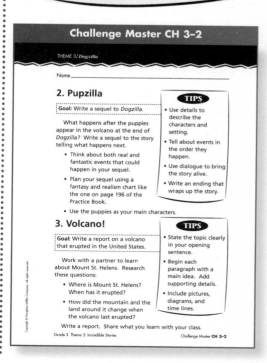

Challenge Master CH 3–2

THEME 3/*Dogzilla*

Name _____

2. Pupzilla

Goal: Write a sequel to *Dogzilla.*

What happens after the puppies appear in the volcano at the end of *Dogzilla?* Write a sequel to the story telling what happens next.

- Think about both real and fantastic events that could happen in your sequel.
- Plan your sequel using a fantasy and realism chart like the one on page 196 of the Practice Book.
- Use the puppies as your main characters.

TIPS
- Use details to describe the characters and setting.
- Tell about events in the order they happen.
- Use dialogue to bring the story alive.
- Write an ending that wraps up the story.

3. Volcano!

Goal: Write a report on a volcano that erupted in the United States.

Work with a partner to learn about Mount St. Helens. Research these questions:

- Where is Mount St. Helens? When has it erupted?
- How did the mountain and the land around it change when the volcano last erupted?

TIPS
- State the topic clearly in your opening sentence.
- Begin each paragraph with a main idea. Add supporting details.
- Include pictures, diagrams, and time lines.

Write a report. Share what you learn with your class.

Grade 3 Theme 3: Incredible Stories

Challenge Master **CH 3–2**

Activities

1. A Long Time Ago 160 MINUTES   INDIVIDUAL

Materials: *art paper, markers, and* **Graphic Organizer Master 3**

DAY 1

Plan Your Folktale

Emphasize to students that a folktale is set in the distant past. Any setting from long ago might be a good source for a story idea.

- Have students choose a landmark they know that seems interesting or mysterious. Students may find it helpful to list ideas or questions they have about this landmark.

- As students begin to develop ideas, have them ask themselves *What if?* questions to generate more ideas about plot and character.

English Language Learners: Allow students to work in pairs. Tell them to write quickly when creating the first draft of their plot without worrying about making mistakes. They should revise word choice and correct grammar later.

DAY 2

Students continue to work on this project.

DAY 3

Write and Draw

Review story maps with students if necessary. Remind them that a folktale has three parts:

- a beginning, which introduces the characters and setting and identifies the problem
- a middle, which tells how the characters try to solve the problem
- an ending, which tells how the problem is solved

DAY 4

Students continue to work on this project.

DAY 5

Share Your Folktale

Explain how folktales have traditionally been passed down from one generation to another by word of mouth. Every storytelling is an exciting performance. Tell students to think about stories their parents have told them. They can tell their own folktales in the same manner if they want.

Challenge Master CH 3–3

THEME 3/*The Mysterious Giant of Barletta*

Name _____

1. A Long Time Ago

Goal: Write a folktale set in a real place.

Plan Your Folktale

Look for ideas for the subject of your folktale in your community and in places around you. Think about
- natural settings like caves, streams, and mountains
- old statues, buildings, and tunnels

Imagine how these places might have been created. Think of stories that might have happened in these places. Write down a few ideas for some folktales.

Write and Draw

Use a story map to list the characters, describe the setting, and write the main plot events. Put them in the order they happen.

Now, write your folktale. Use your story map as your guide. Illustrate the most important scenes.

Share Your Folktale

Decide how you will share your folktale with your classmates. You might:
- Tell your folktale to your classmates. Show your pictures as you tell the story.
- Put your folktale on your class computer or school website.
- Include your story in a class collection of folktales.

TIPS
- Think up a difficult problem, then let your characters solve it.
- Present events in the order they happen.

CH 3–3 Challenge Master   Grade 3 Theme 3: Incredible Stories

---

1

Expected Outcome

A good folktale will include

✔ a difficult problem that is overcome by the main character

✔ events presented in logical order with a beginning, middle, and end

---

2. Charlotte's Web

60 MINUTES   SMALL GROUP   INDIVIDUAL

(Challenge Theme Paperback)

Tell students to practice writing directions as a group. Emphasize that they must give precise directions that instruct the spiders exactly where to begin forming each line of each letter. They must tell them in what direction to spin the line, and how long the line must be. Have students check if they have written good directions by trying to follow them when they are complete.

3. What a Day! 60 MINUTES   INDIVIDUAL

Have students review pages 350–353 of *The Mysterious Giant of Barletta,* which tell of the confrontation between the Mysterious Giant and the invading army. Have them take notes as they review the story. Tell students to try to use details that help the reader see and hear what is happening.

Additional Independent Work
Connecting/Comparing Literature

Have students compare the Leveled Reader selection *The Giant Rock of Yosemite* with the anthology selection *The Mysterious Giant of Barletta,* using what they have learned about Categorize and Classify. Students may discuss or write about their comparisons.

Other Activities

- Challenge Theme Paperback, *Charlotte's Web*
- Theme 3 Assignment Cards 4, 5, 6
- TE p. 349, Word Study
- TE p. 354, Literature Discussion
- TE p. 361, Research Rome
- TE p. 361E, Challenge Word Practice

- TE pp. R6, R11, R19, Challenge
- Education Place: www.eduplace.com More activities related to *The Mysterious Giant of Barletta*
- Accelerated Reader®, *The Mysterious Giant of Barletta*

Expected Outcome

Good directions will include

✔ numbered steps

✔ signal words

✔ precise wording

Expected Outcome

A good journal entry will include

✔ appropriate use of the first person pronouns

✔ details from the point of view of one of the soldiers

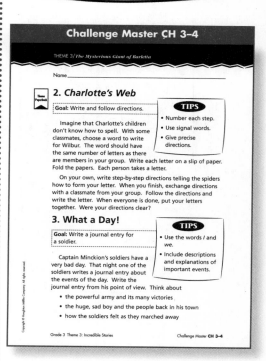

Challenge Master CH 3–4

Activities

Challenge Master CH 3–5

THEME 3/*Raising Dragons*

Name _____

1. A Dragon of Your Own

Goal: Write a story about raising your own dragon.

Plan Your Dragon Tale

Imagine that you find a dragon egg. Now you must figure out how to raise the dragon.

• Reread *Raising Dragons* and look at the pictures for more details and ideas.

• Use a story map to develop a beginning, middle, and end of your story.

Write and Draw

Write the story of raising your dragon. Tell the events in the order that they happen. Describe the setting using sensory details. Present a problem that gets solved. Include dialogue between your characters. Draw two or three pictures that would help tell the story.

TIPS

• Create a plot that has an interesting problem or situation.

• Stick to the main events in your story.

• Use details that help the reader see and hear what is happening.

Share Your Dragon Story

Share your story with others. Use one of these ideas:

• Make the pictures and story into a book. Put the pages together. Make a cover with a picture of you and your dragon. Staple it together. Let your classmates read it.

• Tell your story to a group of classmates. Pass around your pictures as you tell the tale.

CH 3–5 Challenge Master   Grade 3 Theme 3: Incredible Stories

Expected Outcome

A good story will include

✔ a well-developed plot with an interesting problem or situation

✔ a beginning, middle, and end

✔ only events that are necessary to plot development

✔ sensory details that help the reader understand and appreciate the characters, setting, and events

---

1. A Dragon of Your Own

60 MINUTES   INDIVIDUAL

*Materials: art paper, markers, and **Graphic Organizer Master 3***

DAY 1

Plan Your Dragon Tale

Tell students that their dragon will probably be very much like Hank and that they will find a lot of information about raising a dragon in *Raising Dragons*. Remind them to draw conclusions about raising a dragon by looking at the details in the story.

Remind students to introduce the characters, setting, and the basic problem in the beginning of their story. They should tell how the characters deal with the problem in the middle. And they should tell how the problem is solved in the ending.

DAY 2

Students continue to work on this project.

DAY 3

Write and Draw

Check with students on their progress. Then tell students

• to use words that tell about the senses of sight, sound, taste, touch, and smell to describe the characters, setting, and events.

• to make sure that everything that happens in the story is necessary to the plot.

English Language Learners: Tell students to brainstorm sensory details in their primary language and then translate them into English. Suggest that they use a dictionary. Pair them with proficient English speakers during the revision stage.

DAY 4

Students continue to work on this project.

DAY 5

Share Your Dragon Story

Provide opportunities for students to share their stories with classmates. Encourage students to discuss each other's work.

2. When Dragons Grow Up

60 MINUTES INDIVIDUAL

Materials: Graphic Organizer Master 8

- Tell students to use a conclusions chart.
- Have students review the selection to find details that allow them to make conclusions about raising dragons.
- Ask students to state their supporting details when telling their conclusions.
- Have students share their paragraph with the class.

3. News at Six 60 MINUTES PAIR

Students should collaborate to write the news report. Remind students to base their report on information from the story. They should make sure that anything they add or invent is consistent with the story. Provide time for students to read their news report aloud to the class.

Additional Independent Work
Connecting/Comparing Literature

Have students compare the Leveled Reader selection *Driscoll and the Singing Fish* with the anthology selection *Raising Dragons,* using what they have learned about Drawing Conclusions. Students may discuss or write about their comparisons.

Other Activities

- Theme 3 Assignment Cards 7, 8, 9
- TE p. 386, Literature Discussion
- TE p. 393, Research Lizards
- TE p. 393E, Challenge Word Practice

- TE pp. R13, R21, Challenge
- Education Place: www.eduplace.com More activities related to *Raising Dragons*
- Accelerated Reader®, *Raising Dragons*

Expected Outcome

Good conclusions will

✔ be based on accurate supporting details

✔ make sense in terms of the story

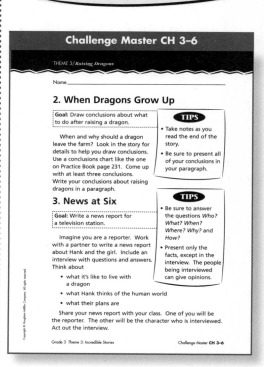

Expected Outcome

A good news report should include

✔ answers to the questions *Who? What? When? Where? Why?* and *How?*

✔ facts only except for opinions that may be volunteered by people being interviewed

1. As Fritz Sees It 160 MINUTES INDIVIDUAL PAIR

Materials: art paper, markers, and **Graphic Organizer Master 3**

DAY 1

Plan Your Story

Have students use the information in *The Garden of Abdul Gasazi* as a starting point for telling the story from Fritz's point of view.

- You may wish to allow students to brainstorm ideas in pairs. They should each take notes and develop their ideas independently.
- Remind students that stories have three main parts: characters, setting, and a plot with a problem the characters must solve.
- If students need a review of story structure, refer them to Practice Book pages 249–250.

English Language Learners: Pair students to review each other's work during the writing process. They will find this particularly useful during revision and the final proofreading stage.

DAY 2

Students continue to work on this project.

DAY 3

Write Your Story

Consult with students on their progress. Provide students with the following ideas:

- Think about how Fritz's personality and character influence his point of view. For example, what does he think of Alan?
- Use sensory details that appeal to the senses of sight and sound.
- Include only characters and events that are necessary to the plot.

DAY 4

Students continue to work on this project.

DAY 5

Share Your Story

Provide opportunities for students to share their stories with classmates. Encourage students to compare and discuss each other's work.

Challenge Master CH 3–7

THEME 3/*The Garden of Abdul Gasazi*

Name _____

1. As Fritz Sees It

Goal: Write the story from Fritz's point of view.

Plan Your Story

Tell the story from Fritz's point of view. Explain what happened after he escaped from Alan.

Brainstorm ideas for your story. Take notes about these questions:

- Did Gasazi capture Fritz?
- Did they really turn Fritz into a duck? If not, where was Fritz and what was he doing?

Organize your story using a story map.

TIPS

- Imagine the problem that Fritz had to solve while Alan was looking for him.
- Tell the events in the order that Fritz experienced them.

Write Your Story

Write Fritz's story. Some parts of the story won't change much. Other parts might be very different. Use your story map as a guide. Think about Fritz. What kind of dog is he? How would he tell the story? Add details that help the reader see and hear what is happening. Draw illustrations to help bring your story to life.

Share Your Story

Share your story with others. You could:

- Read your story to a group of classmates.
- Pass around your pictures while you tell your story to a group of classmates.

CH 3–7 Challenge Master   Grade 3 Theme 3: Incredible Stories

---

1

Expected Outcome

A good story will include

✔ a well-developed plot with a clearly defined problem

✔ events organized in chronological order

✔ details that help the reader understand and appreciate the characters, setting, and events

2. Book Review 60 MINUTES INDIVIDUAL SMALL GROUP

Remind students that a book review tells about a story or book for someone who hasn't read it yet. Have them think, as they write their reviews, about what they would want to know about the story to decide whether or not they want to read it themselves. For additional support, refer students to page 246 of the Practice Book on story structure.

3. Gardens Galore! 60 MINUTES INDIVIDUAL
(Science)
Materials: *art paper, markers, and encyclopedia*

- Tell students to start with an encyclopedia to learn more about the types of gardens.
- Have them use the questions provided, as well as those they generate themselves, to guide their research. Their answers will provide the basis for their reports.
- Tell students to use pictures to help show some of the differences among gardens.

Additional Independent Work
Connecting/Comparing Literature

Have students compare the Leveled Reader selection *A Strange Bird* with the anthology selection *The Garden of Abdul Gasazi*, using what they have learned about Story Structure. Students may discuss or write about their comparisons.

Other Activities

- Theme 3 Assignment Cards 10, 11
- TE p. 412, Literature Discussion
- TE p. 419, Understanding Artistic Style
- TE p. 419E, Challenge Word Practice

- TE pp. R15, R23, Challenge
- Education Place: www.eduplace.com More activities related to *The Garden of Abdul Gasazi*
- Accelerated Reader®, *The Garden of Abdul Gasazi*

2
Expected Outcome
A good book report will include

✔ a description of the characters, setting, and plot

✔ opinions supported by details from the story

✔ a recommendation to readers as to whether or not they should read this story

3
Expected Outcome
A good report will include

✔ a clearly stated topic sentence

✔ facts to support the topic sentence and main ideas

✔ a closing that summarizes the main ideas of the report

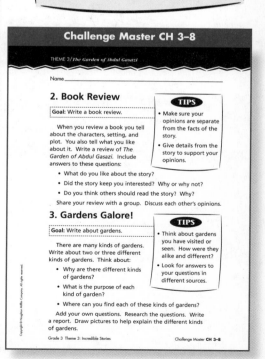

Challenge Master CH 3–8

THEME 3/*The Garden of Abdul Gasazi*

Name _____

2. Book Review

Goal: Write a book review.

When you review a book you tell about the characters, setting, and plot. You also tell what you like about it. Write a review of *The Garden of Abdul Gasazi*. Include answers to these questions:

- What do you like about the story?
- Did the story keep you interested? Why or why not?
- Do you think others should read the story? Why?

Share your review with a group. Discuss each other's opinions.

TIPS
- Make sure your opinions are separate from the facts of the story.
- Give details from the story to support your opinions.

3. Gardens Galore!

Goal: Write about gardens.

There are many kinds of gardens. Write about two or three different kinds of gardens. Think about:

- Why are there different kinds of gardens?
- What is the purpose of each kind of garden?
- Where can you find each of these kinds of gardens?

Add your own questions. Research the questions. Write a report. Draw pictures to help explain the different kinds of gardens.

TIPS
- Think about gardens you have visited or seen. How were they alike and different?
- Look for answers to your questions in different sources.

Grade 3 Theme 3: Incredible Stories   Challenge Master **CH 3–8**

Theme 4

Animal Habitats

Selections

1 Nights of the Pufflings

2 Seal Surfer

3 Two Days in May

1. Animal Habitat Mural

<u>160 MINUTES</u>   INDIVIDUAL   SMALL GROUP

(Science)

Materials: encyclopedia, books about animals, index cards, butcher paper, markers, crayons, paints, tape, and drawing paper

DAY 1

Gather Information

Tell students to pick animals they are interested in learning more about. Remind them to take notes on their animals and habitats for use in the presentation.

English Language Learners: Pair English language learners during planning and research.

DAY 2

Students continue to work on this project.

DAY 3

Draw Your Mural

Check with students on the progress of their murals. Remind students to sketch their drawing and include details from their research. Provide space on the classroom floor or a table for students to draw their mural. Make sure each student has at least three feet of paper.

DAY 4

Students continue to work on this project.

DAY 5

Present Your Mural

Help students hang their murals on the board. Provide class time for them to present their murals.

Challenge Master CH 4–1

THEME 4/ *Nights of the Pufflings*

Name _____

1. Animal Habitat Mural

Goal: Create and present a mural that shows animals in their habitats.

 TIPS
- Be sure to make a sketch of your panel before you draw.
- Present your mural in the order it is drawn.

Gather Information
Working in a small group, brainstorm a list of animals. Have each member of your group look up an animal in an encyclopedia or books on animals. Find out about your animal's habitat. Answer these questions:
- What does the habitat look like?
- What is the animal's home?
- What does the animal eat?
Make notes about your animal and its habitat on index cards.

Draw Your Mural
Plan out your mural panel.
- Draw a sketch of what you want to include in your panel.
- Use the sketches to decide the order of your panels.
- Draw and color your panel on a large sheet of butcher paper.
- Label the animals and plants in your habitat.

Present Your Mural
Hang your mural on the board with tape and present it to the class. Each member of the group should present his or her panel.

CH 4–1 Challenge Master   Grade 3 Theme 4: Animal Habitats

Expected Outcome

A good mural will include

✔ details on the animal and its habitat

✔ well-organized panels

✔ a presentation including information from students' notes

2. Animals Around Us   60 MINUTES   INDIVIDUAL
(Science)

Materials: encyclopedia (optional)

Point out that no matter where they live, students will see wild animals every day. Have students choose one wild animal that is interesting to them and that they have observed with some care. Tell them to write a description of it, using *Nights of the Pufflings* as an example. Emphasize that they should provide as many facts as possible. However, they can also give opinions.

3. Dear Halla   60 MINUTES   INDIVIDUAL
(Social Studies)

Review the parts of a friendly letter. Tell students to keep in mind that Halla might not be familiar with everyday life in the United States. In their letter students may need to explain things to her that they take for granted.

Additional Independent Work
Connecting/Comparing Literature

Have students compare the Leveled Reader selection *Urban Wildlife* with the anthology selection *Nights of the Pufflings,* using what they have learned about Fact and Opinion. Students may discuss or write about their comparisons.

Other Activities

- Theme 4 Assignment Cards 1, 2
- TE p. 32, Literature Discussion
- TE p. 39, Field Guide
- TE p. 39E, Challenge Word Practice

- TE pp. R9, R15, Challenge
- Education Place: www.eduplace.com More activities related to *Nights of the Pufflings*
- Accelerated Reader®, *Nights of the Pufflings*

---

②

Expected Outcome

A good description will include

✔ factual information about the appearance, behavior, and life of the animal

✔ specific, descriptive details

③

Expected Outcome

A good letter will include

✔ all the elements of a friendly letter: heading, greeting, body, closing, and signature

✔ the use of *I* and *we*

✔ an explanation of terms, ideas, and activities that will not be familiar to the reader

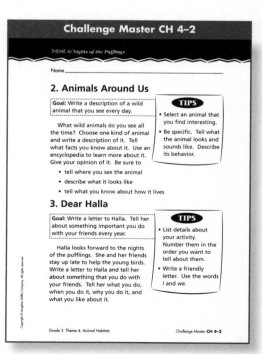

Challenge Master CH 4–2

THEME 4/ *Nights of the Pufflings*

Name _____

2. Animals Around Us

Goal: Write a description of a wild animal that you see every day.

TIPS
- Select an animal that you find interesting.
- Be specific. Tell what the animal looks and sounds like. Describe its behavior.

What wild animals do you see all the time? Choose one kind of animal and write a description of it. Tell what facts you know about it. Use an encyclopedia to learn more about it. Give your opinion of it. Be sure to

- tell where you see the animal
- describe what it looks like
- tell what you know about how it lives

3. Dear Halla

Goal: Write a letter to Halla. Tell her about something important you do with your friends every year.

TIPS
- List details about your activity. Number them in the order you want to tell about them.
- Write a friendly letter. Use the words *I* and *we*.

Halla looks forward to the nights of the pufflings. She and her friends stay up late to help the young birds. Write a letter to Halla and tell her about something that you do with your friends. Tell her what you do, when you do it, why you do it, and what you like about it.

Grade 3 Theme 4: Animal Habitats

Challenge Master **CH 4–2**

Activities

Challenge Master CH 4–3

THEME 4/*Seal Surfer*

Name _____

1. Two Kinds of Seals

Goal: Compare and contrast two kinds of seals.

Gather Information

Did you know there are many kinds of seals? Do research and learn about some of these seals. Pick two kinds of seals to compare and contrast. Think about

- what they look like
- where they live
- how they live

Take Notes

Take notes as you read. Write each main idea at the top of an index card. Write details that tell more about each main idea on each card.

TIPS
- Include only facts about your topic.
- Use illustrations to show the different kinds of seals. Use maps to show where they live.

Compare and Contrast

Use a Venn diagram.

- Label each circle with the names of the two kinds of seals.
- Fill in the center circle with phrases that tell how the seals are alike. Fill in each side circle with phrases that tell how the seals are different.
- Give an oral report to a group of classmates to tell about the seals you picked. Use illustrations and a map to give more information.

CH 4–3 Challenge Master   Grade 3 Theme 4: Animal Habitats

① Expected Outcome

A good activity will include

✔ a clear explanation of the similarities and differences shown in the Venn diagram

✔ the presentation of facts and not opinions

✔ illustrations that show different kinds of seals

---

1. Two Kinds of Seals   160 MINUTES   INDIVIDUAL
(Science)

Materials: encyclopedia, Internet, index cards, art paper, markers, and *Graphic Organizer Master 2*

DAY 1

Gather Information

Refer students to these websites for information on seals:

http://www.terraquest.com/va/science/seals/seals.html

http://www.seaworld.org/Pinnipeds/introduction.html

Remind students to look at headings and subheadings in articles. Remind them that important details can be found in captions and illustrations.

DAY 2

Students continue to work on this project.

DAY 3

Take Notes

Check on students' progress. Tell them to take their notes on index cards. Tell students to write

- one main idea at the top of each card
- details that specifically support each main idea on the same card, beneath the main idea

English Language Learners: Allow students to take notes in their primary language.

DAY 4

Students continue to work on this project.

DAY 5

Compare and Contrast

If necessary, review with students how to use a Venn diagram. Students with strong graphic skills might want to prepare an annotated map. Encourage students to personalize their presentation in some way.

English Language Learners: You may wish to pair students with fluent English speakers for peer editing and proofreading.

2. Surfing   60 MINUTES   INDIVIDUAL
(Social Studies)

Materials: encyclopedia, art paper, and markers

- Tell students they can limit their reports to a specific aspect of surfing, such as where people surf, types of surfing, or skills needed.

- You may wish to review types of organization with students. Order of importance may be most appropriate for explanatory paragraphs if, for example, students are explaining where or why people surf. Time order might be used if students are explaining how to surf.

3. *In Good Hands*   60 MINUTES   INDIVIDUAL   SMALL GROUP
(Challenge Theme Paperback)
(Social Studies) (Science)

You may want to recommend additional reading on the topic of people working to save animals and plants. *Someday a Tree* from the Houghton Mifflin Social Studies Bookshelf is one possibility.

Additional Independent Work
Connecting/Comparing Literature

Have students compare the Leveled Reader selection *Hometown Turtles* with the anthology selection *Seal Surfer*, using what they have learned about Compare and Contrast. Students may discuss or write about their comparisons.

Other Activities

- Challenge Theme Paperback, *In Good Hands*
- Theme 4 Assignment Cards 3, 4, 5
- TE p. 62, Literature Discussion
- TE p. 69, Careers
- TE p. 69E, Challenge Word Practice

- TE pp. R6, R11, R17, Challenge
- Education Place: www.eduplace.com More activities related to *Seal Surfer*
- Accelerated Reader®, *Seal Surfer*

---

②

Expected Outcome

A good report will include

✔ a clearly stated topic sentence

✔ specific, descriptive details

③

Expected Outcome

A good discussion will include

✔ opinions that are well-supported by facts and details from *In Good Hands* and other sources

✔ listening carefully to classmates' opinions and considering them seriously

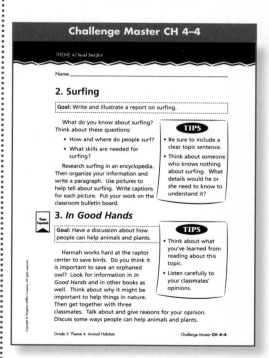

Activities

① Expected Outcome

A good presentation will include

✔ facts that clearly describe the problem

✔ a well-considered solution

✔ strong reasons and facts to support opinions and the solution

1. Nowhere to Go   160 MINUTES   INDIVIDUAL
(Science) (Social Studies)

Materials: encyclopedia, books on animals, and articles on the environment from children's magazines, such as Ranger Rick *or* National Geographic World

DAY 1

Gather Information

- Urge students to talk to family members and neighbors who may have knowledge about habitat loss. Students should also include any first-hand knowledge or experience they have as they gather information on the topic.

- Tell students to take careful notes, jotting down main ideas and supporting details. They can use index cards or an outline format for note taking.

English Language Learners: Allow students to take notes in their primary language. Tell them to collect vocabulary words as they read to prepare to write about and discuss their subject.

DAY 2

Students continue to work on this project.

DAY 3

Think About the Problem

Check-in with students to see how well they are progressing. If necessary, review the use of a problem-and-solution chart, such as the one on TE page 87. Emphasize that the chart will help them analyze and compare different solutions to find the best choice. Point out that sometimes the best solution is a combination of alternatives.

DAY 4

Students continue to work on this project.

DAY 5

Share Your Information

Encourage students to develop their own ideas for sharing the information they've gathered and the solutions they've chosen. Provide class time for students to present their work and share ideas.

2. In My Opinion . . .   <u>60 MINUTES</u> INDIVIDUAL

(Science) (Social Studies)

Materials: articles on the environment from children's magazines, such as Ranger Rick *or* National Geographic World

Refer students to Practice Book page 39 to develop their decision chart. Remind students that there may be more than one correct decision since opinions are involved. Emphasize they should provide strong evidence to support their opinions.

3. *Two Days in May*   <u>60 MINUTES</u> INDIVIDUAL

(Challenge Theme Paperback)

Remind students that since they are writing a first-person narrative, they should use the pronoun *I*. Tell them to include the same events that occur in *Two Days in May*. Point out that the deer might experience these events differently from the way Sonia does. Encourage students to imagine additional events, such as what happened before or after the events related in *Two Days in May*.

Additional Independent Work

Connecting/Comparing Literature ⭐

Have students compare the Leveled Reader selection *Poor Little Kittens* with the anthology selection *Two Days in May*, using what they have learned about Making Judgments. Students may discuss or write about their comparisons.

Other Activities

- Challenge Theme Paperback, *Two Days in May*
- Theme 4 Assignment Cards 6, 7, 8
- TE p. 92, Literature Discussion
- TE p. 99, Writing Poetry
- TE p. 99E, Challenge Words Practice

- TE pp. R6, R13, R19, Challenge
- Education Place: www.eduplace.com More activities related to *Two Days in May*
- Accelerated Reader®, *Two Days in May*

---

❷ Expected Outcome

A good opinion essay will include

✔ a clearly stated opinion

✔ supporting reasons and facts

✔ a conclusion that restates the writer's opinion and summarizes reasons

❸ Expected Outcome

A good story will include

✔ an engaging beginning,

✔ details that tell what the deer saw, heard, and felt

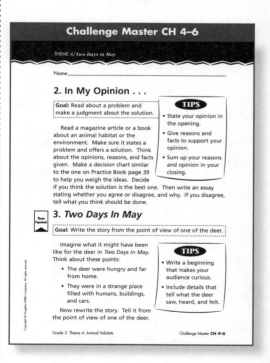

Theme 5

Voyagers

Selections

1 Across the Wide Dark Sea

2 Yunmi and Halmoni's Trip

3 Trapped by the Ice!

Activities

Challenge Master CH 5-1

THEME 5/*Across the Wide Dark Sea*

Name _____

1. A Story About Squanto

Goal: Write historical fiction that tells about an important visitor to the Pilgrims' settlement.

Gather Information
Use an encyclopedia or another reference source to learn more about Squanto. Take notes.

Write Your Story
Choose one time in Squanto's life to tell about. Build your story around that event. Use a story map to organize your ideas.

- Describe the setting.
- Develop your plot. Begin with a real problem that Squanto faced. Add events that tell how he tried to solve the problem.
- Add realistic details. Tell what the characters think and feel.

Put it together and write your story.

Share Your Historical Fiction
Decide how you want to share your story. You might:
- Create an illustrated book.
- Read or tell your story aloud to a group of classmates.
- Post your story on the classroom computer.

TIPS
- Stick to the facts from your research.
- Use real people from that time as characters, if possible.

CH 5-1 Challenge Master   Grade 3 Theme 5: Voyagers

Expected Outcome

A good story will include

✔ a plot that has a beginning, a middle, an end, and a problem that is solved

✔ events that contribute directly to the plot and that are in a sensible order

✔ realistic, consistent details and dialogue

1. A Story About Squanto

I 50 MINUTES   INDIVIDUAL

(Social Studies)

Materials: *encyclopedia and* ***Graphic Organizer Master 3***

DAY 1

Gather Information

Tell students that they are reading historical fiction. This is a kind of fiction that uses real, historical people and events. The dialogue, thoughts, and details that the author writes are made up. An author of historical fiction does careful research so that the story could really have happened. Now students will write their own historical fiction. Tell them to do research in two stages.

- First, they should read an encyclopedia article about Squanto to learn the general facts of his life. From this research they can choose an episode on which to base their story.

- In the second stage, they should think about other events that will complete their story.

DAY 2

Students continue to work on this project.

DAY 3

Write Your Story

Check in with your students on the progress of their research and story development. Have them limit their story to one event so that they can develop it fully. Tell students that historical fiction has all the elements of a story: characters, setting, and plot.

English Language Learners: Tell students to brainstorm a list of sight, sound, touch, and taste details to use in describing the setting and events. They might list them in their primary language and then translate them. Have them use the list as a resource as they write.

DAY 4

Students continue to work on this project.

DAY 5

Share Your Historical Fiction

Tell students to share their work in the way that is most enjoyable to them. You may want to provide classroom time for students to discuss the historical basis for their stories in addition to presenting them.

2. Our First Conversation 60 MINUTES INDIVIDUAL
(Social Studies)

If necessary, review with students the format of a dialogue. Remind them that when they make an inference, they use clues from the story plus personal knowledge to make guesses about the characters, setting, and events that the author has not included. Suggest that students first read their completed dialogue aloud to themselves. It should sound like two different people talking.

3. Journey in Time 60 MINUTES INDIVIDUAL

Remind students to brainstorm ideas and take notes before they begin writing.

Additional Independent Work
Connecting/Comparing Literature

Have students compare the Leveled Reader selection *Faith's Journey* with the anthology selection *Across the Wide Dark Sea,* using what they have learned about Making Inferences. Students may discuss or write about their comparisons.

Other Activities

- Theme 5 Assignment Cards 1, 2, 3
- TE p. 176, Literature Discussion
- TE p. 183, Research Skills
- TE p. 183E, Challenge Word Practice

- TE pp. R9, R15, Challenge
- Education Place: www.eduplace.com
  More activities related to *Across the Wide Dark Sea*
- Accelerated Reader®, *Across the Wide Dark Sea*

2

Expected Outcome

A good dialogue will include

✔ realistic, conversational language

✔ the name of each character followed by a colon

✔ a consistent voice for each character—identity, language, tone

---

3

Expected Outcome

A good narrative will include

✔ an opening sentence that captures the audience's attention

✔ a first-person point of view

✔ sensory details that tell what the narrator saw, heard, or felt

---

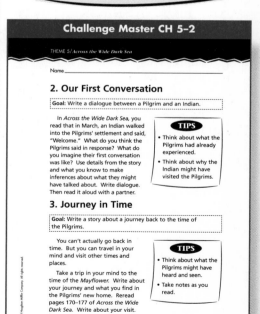

Challenge Master CH 5–2

THEME 5/*Across the Wide Dark Sea*

Name _____

2. Our First Conversation

Goal: Write a dialogue between a Pilgrim and an Indian.

In *Across the Wide Dark Sea,* you read that in March, an Indian walked into the Pilgrims' settlement and said, "Welcome." What do you think the Pilgrims said in response? What do you imagine their first conversation was like? Use details from the story and what you know to make inferences about what they might have talked about. Write dialogue. Then read it aloud with a partner.

TIPS
- Think about what the Pilgrims had already experienced.
- Think about why the Indian might have visited the Pilgrims.

3. Journey in Time

Goal: Write a story about a journey back to the time of the Pilgrims.

You can't actually go back in time. But you can travel in your mind and visit other times and places.

Take a trip in your mind to the time of the *Mayflower.* Write about your journey and what you find in the Pilgrims' new home. Reread pages 170–177 of *Across the Wide Dark Sea.* Write about your visit.

TIPS
- Think about what the Pilgrims might have heard and seen.
- Take notes as you read.

Grade 3 Theme 5: Voyagers

Challenge Master **CH 5–2**

Activities

Expected Outcome

A good travel guide will include

✔ a logical organization

✔ helpful headings and subheadings

✔ specific details

✔ effective use of maps and illustrations

---

1. Travel Guide 150 MINUTES INDIVIDUAL
(Social Studies)

Materials: Graphic Organizer Master 4, encyclopedia, Atlas, Internet, drawing paper and markers (optional)

DAY 1

Gather Information

• Tell students to begin with general research about places in Korea. Then they should narrow their search and focus on gathering information about a few specific sites. Refer them to http://www.knto.or.kr/english for tourist information about Korea.

• Students will find the K-W-L chart most useful after they have narrowed their search. Explain that it will help them focus their research so they know exactly what information they need.

English Language Learners: Have students work in pairs for the assignment. You might suggest that they plan a presentation that relies heavily on maps and illustrations.

DAY 2

Students continue to work on this project.

DAY 3

Write Your Travel Guide

Check with students on the progress of their research. Emphasize the need for them to limit their travel guides to a few sites they would like to visit. You may wish to review your organization of information with students. Tell them to consider organizing their guides according to

• geographic location
• categories such as museums, historic sites, or natural features

DAY 4

Students continue to work on this project.

DAY 5

Share Your Travel Guide

Tell students to share their information in a format that they are most comfortable with. For example, a bulletin board display may be more suitable for students with strong graphic skills, or students who enjoy writing may prefer to create a brochure.

2. Will You Visit? 60 MINUTES INDIVIDUAL

Remind students of the steps in making successful predictions. Refer them to page 106 of the Practice Book for additional help with this skill. Have students review the selection to gather useful clues.

3. *Balto and the Great Race*

60 MINUTES INDIVIDUAL

(Challenge Theme Paperback)

Students will need to read an additional story about animals to do this activity. Remind students that they should both compare and contrast the two stories and express their opinions about them.

Additional Independent Work

Connecting/Comparing Literature

Have students compare the Leveled Reader selection *The Same, But Different* with the anthology selection *Yunmi and Halmoni's Trip*, using what they have learned about Predicting Outcomes. Students may discuss or write about their comparisons.

Other Activities

- Challenge Theme Paperback, *Balto and the Great Race*
- Theme 5 Assignment Cards 4, 5, 6
- TE p. 206, Literature Discussion
- TE p. 213, Research Skills
- TE p. 213E, Challenge Word Practice

- TE pp. R6, R11, R17, Challenge
- Education Place: www.eduplace.com More activities related to *Yunmi and Halmoni's Trip*
- Accelerated Reader®, *Yunmi and Halmoni's Trip*

2

Expected Outcome

A good story will include

✔ a plot that has a beginning, a middle, and an end

✔ characters who are trying to solve a problem

✔ details and dialogue that make the plot, characters, and setting interesting

3

Expected Outcome

A good essay will include

✔ an introduction that names the two stories

✔ examples and reasons to support statements

✔ a conclusion that sums up the important points

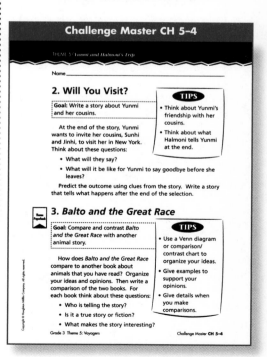

1. The Arctic and Antarctica

150 MINUTES   INDIVIDUAL   PAIR

(Social Studies) (Science)

Materials: Graphic Organizer Master 2, encyclopedia, markers, and art paper (optional)

DAY 1

Find the Facts

Tell students they are to become classroom experts on the most northern and southern parts of the earth. Have them use the following steps:

- Think about what kinds of information are important to gather to make a good comparison of the two regions.
- Write facts that they might already know in their diagrams before they begin their research. Then check these facts for accuracy as they read.

English Language Learners: Use a globe to help students understand that the term *polar regions* refers to the areas surrounding the North and South Poles.

DAY 2

Students continue to work on this project.

DAY 3

Compare the Facts

Check with students on the progress of their information gathering. Remind them that their goals are to compare and contrast the two regions. To compare and contrast any two things, it is necessary to have information about the same qualities or characteristics of each.

DAY 4

Students continue to work on this project.

DAY 5

Share What You Know

Tell students to choose a presentation format that will clearly showcase all that they have learned. If desired, students may combine two formats.

Challenge Master CH 5–5

THEME 5/*Trapped by the Ice!*

Name _____

1. The Arctic and Antarctica

Goal: Compare and contrast the Arctic with Antarctica.

TIPS
- Focus on *comparing* and *contrasting*.
- Organize your information so it is easy to read. Use headings, titles, captions, and labels.

Find the Facts

Many people get Antarctica confused with the Arctic.

- Use a Venn diagram. Label one circle *Antarctica*, the other *Arctic*, and the overlapping area *Both*.
- Fill in facts that you already know about Antarctica from reading *Trapped by the Ice!*
- Use an encyclopedia to find facts about the Arctic. What lives there? What are the summer and winter temperatures?
- Fill in any facts that apply to both regions.

Compare the Facts

Read the information in your diagram. What else would you like to find out? Use an encyclopedia to find other information for both the Arctic and Antarctica, such as any explorers who have visited the regions.

Share What You Know

Decide how to present your information. You could:

- Write a report.
- Make a "picture essay." Draw several pictures and write captions to show what you have learned.
- Give an oral presentation to the class.

CH 5–5 Challenge Master   Grade 3 Theme 5: Voyagers

---

①

Expected Outcome

A good comparison/contrast analysis will include

✔ inclusion of details about the polar regions

✔ focus on similarities and differences between the two polar regions

✔ clear presentation, including the use of text organization wherever possible

2. What's in a Name? <u>60 MINUTES</u> INDIVIDUAL PAIR
Materials: *dictionary*

Tell students to start by checking the dictionary for the meaning of the word *endurance,* and then write a definition in their own words. Have students review the selection to find details and events that help them form an opinion and support their reasoning.

3. A Crew Member's Letter

<u>60 MINUTES</u> INDIVIDUAL

Tell students to imagine what it was like to be under Shackleton's leadership. Then tell students to write a personal letter such as a crew member would send to a friend or a family member, once they had reached safety.

Additional Independent Work
Connecting/Comparing Literature

Have students compare the Leveled Reader selection *Voyage Across the Pacific* with the anthology selection *Trapped by the Ice!,* using what they have learned about Text Organization. Students may discuss or write about their comparisons.

Other Activities

- Theme 5 Assignment Cards 7, 8, 9
- TE p. 244, Literature Discussion
- TE p. 251, A Photo Essay
- TE p. 251E, Challenge Word Practice
- TE p. R13, R19, Challenge

- Education Place: www.eduplace.com More activities related to *Trapped by the Ice!*
- Accelerated Reader®, *Trapped by the Ice!*

2

Expected Outcome

A good paragraph will include

- ✔ a demonstrated understanding of the meaning of the word *endurance*
- ✔ a clearly stated opinion
- ✔ references to story events, details, and actions that support the student's stated opinion

3

Expected Outcome

A good letter will include

- ✔ writing from a crew member's point of view
- ✔ inclusion of story details that show aspects of Shackleton's character
- ✔ correct letter format, including a heading, greeting, body, closing, and signature

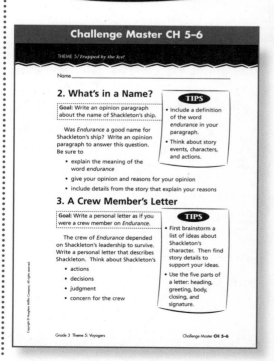

Challenge Master CH 5–6

Theme 6

Smart Solutions

Selections

1 Pepita Talks Twice

2 Poppa's New Pants

3 Ramona Quimby, Age 8

Activities

Expected Outcome

A good comic strip will include

✔ a clearly identifiable problem and solution

✔ well-defined, clearly ordered steps

✔ obvious connections between all steps in the process

1. Smart Comic Strip Solutions

<u>160 MINUTES</u>   PAIR

Materials: *poster board, drawing paper, and markers*

DAY 1

Choose a Problem and Plan a Solution

- Tell students to turn to page 296. Explain that they will create a comic strip showing a similarly complex and amusing solution to a simple everyday problem. Their strips should have some text as well as pictures.
- Tell students they might find it easiest to begin with the final step in the process. First, they can think of a clever way to get that last task done. Then work backward to the beginning.

DAY 2

Students continue to work on this project.

DAY 3

Create Your Comic Strip

Tell students that their strips should follow the steps they identified in their cause-effect chart.

DAY 4

Students continue to work on this project.

DAY 5

Share Your Comic Strip

Tell students to choose the format that best fits their solution. Some solutions might be better illustrated by a series of boxes. Other solutions may be better illustrated in a single frame. Encourage students to take their completed comic strip solutions home after presenting them to the class.

2. Problems, Problems, Problems

60 MINUTES   INDIVIDUAL

Materials: Three Days on a Red River in a Red Cave, How the Stars Fell into the Sky, *and Graphic Organizer Master 6*

- Students will need to have read another book in order to have a problem and decision to evaluate. This book might come from the Social Studies Bookshelf or it might be another book or story students have read.

- Tell students that they should evaluate the characters' decision in their essays, but that they may propose their own solution if they think it is better. They should provide reasons to support their evaluation.

3. In My Opinion   60 MINUTES   INDIVIDUAL

Have students look at what their character does and says to find clues to what solution the character would suggest to Pepita for her problem. You might refer students to the Character Chart on Practice Book page 106 for help in making predictions and inferences. Emphasize that students' letters to Pepita should sound like they were written by the characters they chose.

Additional Independent Work
Connecting/Comparing Literature

Have students compare the Leveled Reader selection *Paul the Artist* with the anthology selection *Pepita Talks Twice*, using what they have learned about Problem Solving. Students may discuss or write about their comparisons.

Other Activities

- Theme 6 Assignment Cards 1, 2, 3
- TE p. 313, Word Choice
- TE p. 330, Literature Discussion
- TE p. 337, Music
- TE p. 337E, Challenge Word Practice

- TE pp. R9, R15, Challenge
- Education Place: www.eduplace.com More activities related to *Pepita Talks Twice*
- Accelerated Reader®, *Pepita Talks Twice*

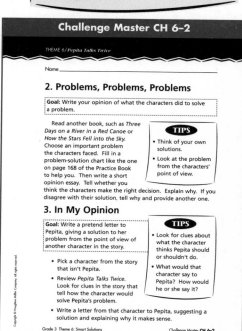

②

Expected Outcome

A good essay will include

✔ an opening that states the problem and the student's opinion of the solution

✔ an evaluation of the decisions made by the characters

✔ a proposed solution, which may or may not be the same as that of the characters

③

Expected Outcome

A good opinion letter will include

✔ a clear statement of the problem

✔ a suggested solution with supporting reasons and details

✔ a heading, greeting, body, closing, and signature

Activities

---

1. It Was So Funny . . . 160 MINUTES INDIVIDUAL

DAY 1

Plan Your Funny Story

To help students develop ideas and plan their stories:

- Have them begin by forming groups to brainstorm funny experiences they have had. Tell them to write down ideas to use later.
- Suggest that they draw a picture of an important scene from their story. The drawing may help them think of more details.
- Tell them to identify what makes their story funny.

DAY 2

Students continue to work on this project.

DAY 3

Write Your Story

Check with students on their progress with their stories. Remind them that their stories should have a setting, characters, a problem, major events, and a solution to the problem. Tell students to use a story map to organize the various elements of their story.

DAY 4

Students continue to work on this project.

DAY 5

Share Your Story

Encourage students to choose the format for sharing their story they like best. If students present their stories orally, remind them that they should sound as if they were telling their story to their friends.

Challenge Master CH 6–3

THEME 6/*Poppa's New Pants*

Name_____

1. It Was So Funny . . .

Goal: Write a story about a funny personal experience.

Plan Your Funny Story

Think of a time when you saw or experienced something really funny. Then gather details. Take notes as you think about

- what happened
- where and when it happened
- who was there

Then make a story map. Fill in the details telling what you saw, heard, and felt.

TIPS

- Tell your story from your point of view.
- Use specific details.
- Use exaggeration to add humor.

Write Your Story

Your story should have a beginning, a middle, and an end. When you write

- introduce your characters at the beginning of the story
- tell events in the order they happened
- write an ending that wraps up the story
- include dialogue to define the characters and move the action along
- include all the humorous elements in your plot

Share Your Story

Share your story with your classmates. Use one of these ideas.

- Post your story on your class computer or school website.
- Make your story into a book by adding drawings.
- Practice telling your story aloud. Then tell it to the class.

CH 6–3 Challenge Master   Grade 3 Theme 6: Smart Solutions

1

Expected Outcome

A good funny story will include

✔ a catchy opening that gets readers interested right away

✔ a well-developed and organized plot told in a distinctive, personal voice

✔ sensory details that help the reader know and appreciate the characters, setting, and events

✔ effective use of exaggeration and unexpected events

2. Grandma Tiny Speaks 60 MINUTES INDIVIDUAL

Tell students that when they make inferences about Grandma Tiny, they can rely on their personal knowledge of people as well as details they get from the story. Suggest that students can develop their story by first writing a dialogue between Grandma Tiny and one of her relatives or a friend. They can then turn the dialogue into a straight personal narrative.

3. *Stealing Home* 60 MINUTES INDIVIDUAL
(Challenge Theme Paperback)

Remind students that in order to draw conclusions about the authors' viewpoints, they must look in the books for details that help explain what the authors don't tell directly. In their essays, students should present the authors' viewpoints and tell how they reached their conclusions.

Additional Independent Work
Connecting/Comparing Literature

Have students compare the Leveled Reader selection *Gampy's Lamps* with the anthology selection *Poppa's New Pants*, using what they have learned about Drawing Conclusions. Students may discuss or write about their comparisons.

Other Activities

- Challenge Theme Paperback, *Stealing Home*
- Theme 6 Assignment Cards 4, 5, 6
- TE p. 359, Humor
- TE p. 360, Literature Discussion
- TE p. 367, Original Comics
- TE p. 367E, Challenge Word Practice

- TE pp. R6, R11, R17, Challenge
- Education Place: www.eduplace.com More activities related to *Poppa's New Pants*
- Accelerated Reader®, *Poppa's New Pants*

Expected Outcome

A good story will include

- ✔ an introduction to the characters, setting, and problem
- ✔ an explanation of how the characters deal with the problem
- ✔ events in the correct order
- ✔ details that make the story interesting

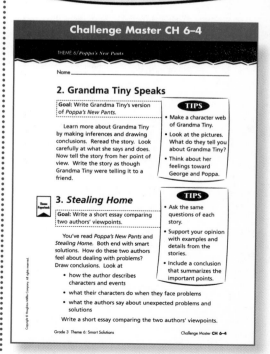

Expected Outcome

A good essay will include

- ✔ a clearly stated opinion
- ✔ strong reasons and details from the books to support their opinion
- ✔ a conclusion that summarizes important points

Activities

Challenge Master CH 6–5

Name

1. Another Sunday

Goal: Write a story about another Sunday when the Quimbys meet the old man again.

TIPS
- Use dialogue.
- Include details that show what your characters see, hear, and feel.
- Make sure your characters act and talk the way they did in the original story.

Plan Your Story

Write a story about another time the Quimbys meet the old man. Think about what might happen.
- Where might the Quimbys meet the old man again?
- What do you think they would say or ask each other?
- How would they feel?

Come up with several possible answers to each question. Based on the story, which of your answers are most possible?

Write Your Story

Before you begin writing, complete a story map. Use the map to guide you as you write. Describe the setting and characters. Decide on a problem and how the characters will solve it. Decide on the order of the major events in your story. Now write your story.

Share Your Story

Decide how you want to share your story. You could:
- Read your story aloud to a group of classmates.
- Publish your story on your class computer or website.
- Make a collection of classroom stories. Put all your stories together. Make a cover.

CH 6–5 Challenge Master   Grade 3 Theme 6: Smart Solutions

---

❶ Expected Outcome

A good story will include

✔ a strong beginning that makes the reader want to know what will happen

✔ an interesting problem that motivates the characters to some action

✔ a series of events that develop in logical order

✔ sensory details that enable the reader to picture the characters, setting, and events

---

1. Another Sunday   160 MINUTES   INDIVIDUAL

Materials: Graphic Organizer Master 3

DAY 1

Plan Your Story

Tell students to spend time exploring ideas for their story rather than choosing the first idea that comes to them. If they have trouble generating ideas, suggest that they ask themselves *What if* questions. For example: What if they meet at Whopperburger again as they wait for a table? What if Mr. Quimby asks the man to join them for dinner?

DAY 2

Students continue to work on this project.

DAY 3

Write Your Story

Check with students on their progress with their stories. Remind students that their stories should have a beginning, middle, and an end. Tell students to include dialogue and interesting details that give insight to the characters.

English Language Learners: Tell students to write their stories without stopping to search for words in the dictionary. If they want, they can leave some words in their primary language. As they revise their work, they can look for the exact words they want in English.

DAY 4

Students continue to work on this project.

DAY 5

Share Your Story

Encourage students to find original ways to share their stories. If they decide on oral presentations, tell them to prepare by reading the story aloud to themselves and experimenting with expression.

2. Beverly Cleary's Books

60 MINUTES   INDIVIDUAL   SMALL GROUP

*Materials: other books by Beverly Cleary and **Graphic Organizer Master 9***

Encourage each student to read a different book by Cleary. When students get together in groups, they should select someone to take notes and fill in a generalization chart at the group's direction. You might also have groups share their generalizations with the class.

3. Book Review   60 MINUTES   INDIVIDUAL

Tell students to evaluate the story elements—characters, setting, and plot—as part of their review. They should also analyze the pictures. Tell them to think about whether they like the pictures and also how well the pictures illustrate and help tell the story. Students should conclude their reviews with a recommendation regarding the book, giving reasons for their recommendation. Have students post their reviews on the Education Place website at http://www.eduplace.com/kids under the section "KidViews."

Additional Independent Work
Connecting/Comparing Literature

Have students compare the Leveled Reader selection *Real Team Soccer* with the anthology selection *Ramona Quimby, Age 8,* using what they have learned about Making Generalizations. Students may discuss or write about their comparisons.

Other Activities

- Theme 6 Assignment Cards 7, 8, 9
- TE p. 392, Literature Discussion
- TE p. 399, Perform a Play
- TE p. 399E, Challenge Word Practice

- TE pp. R13, R19, Challenge
- Education Place: www.eduplace.com More activities related to *Ramona Quimby, Age 8*
- Accelerated Reader®, *Ramona Quimby, Age 8*

---

②

Expected Outcome

A good book discussion will include

✔ ideas and opinions supported by examples from the books

✔ equal participation by all members of the group

✔ a clear list of generalizations about books by Cleary

③

Expected Outcome

A good book review will include

✔ clearly stated opinions

✔ strong reasons and details from the book to support the opinions

✔ a conclusion that summarizes important points

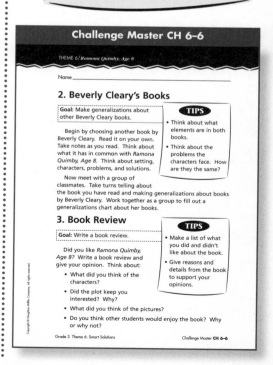

Challenge Master CH 6–6

THEME 6/*Ramona Quimby, Age 8*

Name _____

2. Beverly Cleary's Books

Goal: Make generalizations about other Beverly Cleary books.

Begin by choosing another book by Beverly Cleary. Read it on your own. Take notes as you read. Think about what it has in common with *Ramona Quimby, Age 8.* Think about setting, characters, problems, and solutions.

Now meet with a group of classmates. Take turns telling about the book you have read and making generalizations about books by Beverly Cleary. Work together as a group to fill out a generalizations chart about her books.

TIPS
- Think about what elements are in both books.
- Think about the problems the characters face. How are they the same?

3. Book Review

Goal: Write a book review.

Did you like *Ramona Quimby, Age 8?* Write a book review and give your opinion. Think about:

- What did you think of the characters?
- Did the plot keep you interested? Why?
- What did you think of the pictures?
- Do you think other students would enjoy the book? Why or why not?

TIPS
- Make a list of what you did and didn't like about the book.
- Give reasons and details from the book to support your opinions.

Grade 3 Theme 6: Smart Solutions   Challenge Master **CH 6–6**

Blackline Masters for Grade 3

Activity Masters
Graphic Organizer Masters

Name _____

1. How High Can You Climb?

Goal: Give an oral report on rock climbing.

Gather Details

Reread pages 28–32 of *Cliff Hanger*.

- Fill in a K-W-L chart about rock climbing. Fill in facts you know from the story and from your own experience.

- Brainstorm a list of questions you'd like answered. For example, *What kinds of rock climbing are there?*

- Begin research. Check the encyclopedia, magazines, or other reference sources.

- Work on your chart, adding facts and questions as you go.

Prepare Notes About Climbing

- Make an outline of your main ideas.

- Write notes on index cards. Follow your outline, and use your K-W-L chart.

- Use visual aids such as pictures, maps, or charts.

> **TIPS**
> - Focus on ways to learn safe rock climbing skills.
> - Make drawings or diagrams to illustrate your ideas.

Share What You Know

Tell your classmates what you have learned.

- Look directly at your audience. Speak loudly, clearly, and not too fast.

- Practice using your visual aids. Be sure letters on posters and charts are large enough for the audience to see.

2. Book Talk

Goal: Discuss adventure books.

TIPS

- Compare your book to other books or stories your classmates have read.
- Do not tell too much about the plot. Let others discover it for themselves.

Meet with a group and discuss your favorite adventure books. Before you meet, plan ahead what you will say about your book. Think about questions like these:

- Why do you like the book?

- Who are the main characters? Do you like them? Why?

- What is one paragraph you could share with the group?

When others present books, ask questions.

3. Dag's Story

Goal: Rewrite *Cliff Hanger* from Dag's point of view.

TIPS

- Read the story again. Take notes about Dag.
- How is Dag's point of view different from his son's? Why?

Rewrite the part of the story that tells about the climb from Dag's point of view. Think about these questions:

- Why does Dag change his mind about letting Axel climb the mountain?

- What was Dag thinking as he watched Axel descend? Why did he say, "That was so close, I can't talk about it"?

- How does Dag feel when Axel safely reaches the bottom of the mountain?

Name _____

1. *Mulan:* The Play

Goal: Rewrite the legend of Mulan as a play and perform it.

Start Gathering Details

- List the characters in *The Ballad of Mulan* and describe them. Use an inference chart like the one on page 32 of the Practice Book to help you.

- Note details about the setting.

- List each of the events in the order in which they happen.

- Take notes of dialogue and actions you want to use.

Now plan what you'll use in your play. What events will you show or tell about? How many characters will you use?

Begin Writing

Remember, you have to tell the whole story through dialogue. *Dialogue* is what actors say to each other. Write dialogue that sounds real. Sometimes you will have a change in time or place. Have your actors leave the stage briefly to mark the end of a scene.

TIPS

- Don't use too many locations for your play.

- Keep each piece of dialogue short.

Perform the Play

Present your play to your class. First give a reading of the play. Allow classmates to read the different parts. Read the play aloud, but don't act it out. Gather your actors and choose actions to go along with the dialogue. Rehearse the play the way you want it to be. Make some basic costumes from cardboard, paper, or other materials. Now perform the play.

Name_____

Theme Paperback

2. *Abigail's Drum*

Goal: Write a paragraph about lighthouses.

Do research to learn more about lighthouses. Compare Scituate Lighthouse in *Abigail's Drum* to other lighthouses. Think about these questions:

- How is Scituate Lighthouse like other lighthouses?

- How important were lighthouses and are they still useful?

TIPS

- Compare lighthouses by telling how they are alike and different.

- Use drawings to show details about lighthouses.

Name_____

Theme Paperback

2. *Abigail's Drum*

Goal: Write a paragraph about lighthouses.

Do research to learn more about lighthouses. Compare Scituate Lighthouse in *Abigail's Drum* to other lighthouses. Think about these questions:

- How is Scituate Lighthouse like other lighthouses?

- How important were lighthouses and are they still useful?

TIPS

- Compare lighthouses by telling how they are alike and different.

- Use drawings to show details about lighthouses.

Name _____

1. My Unusual Adventure

Goal: Gather ideas and write a story about an unusual adventure.

Explore for Ideas

- Look at pictures of places in encyclopedias, magazines, or books. Pick some favorite ones.

- Imagine that something strange is hidden from view.

- Choose one picture as the setting of your story.

- Write some notes about what your story might be about.

TIPS

- Write *dialogue*—the words that the characters say to each other. Put quotation marks (" ") around their words.

- Describe your characters. Tell what they look like, how they act, or what they're feeling and thinking.

Begin Writing

Read your notes. Organize and develop your ideas. Then write your story.

- Think about the plot, or what happens in the story. Write the events in the order in which they will happen.

- Describe the place. Think about what you see, hear, feel, smell, and taste.

Share What You Know

Decide how to share your story. You might:

- Read your story aloud to the class.

- Work with classmates to put all your stories together in one book. Place the book in your class library.

2. Wait Until You Hear This!

Goal: Give a short oral presentation as one of the characters from *The Lost and Found.*

TIPS

- Reread *The Lost and Found* and list all the major events.
- Number the events in the order they happened.
- Use your list to organize your presentation.

Choose Mona, Wendell, or Floyd as a character you would like to role-play. Prepare a short presentation telling about one of your adventures in *The Lost and Found.* Tell about events in the order in which they happened.

- Pick the most important events.
- Use words like *first, next, a few minutes later, then,* and *at last.* They will help the audience know the order of events.
- Use as much expression in your voice as possible.

3. There It Is!

Goal: Write a personal letter to ask about something you have lost.

- Brainstorm a story of how you lost the item.
- List questions you need answered in order to find the item.

Suppose that you saw something of yours in a picture in *The Lost and Found.* Write a friendly letter to one of the characters in the book asking about the item.

- Ask if he or she saw the item.
- Tell them how you lost it.
- Get directions for finding your way in the bin.

Name_____

1. My Treasure Story

Goal: Write and illustrate a story about a family treasure.

Gather Details

Start by thinking about something that has special meaning and reminds you of family or friends. Use a cluster map to organize ideas. Write the name of the object in the middle circle. In the surrounding circles write names of people it reminds you of, celebrations that you think of, and any other memories.

Write and Draw

Pick the most important ideas from your maps to write about. When writing:

- Tell about events in order.
- Add details that tell what people see, hear, and feel.
- Choose events to illustrate.

Share Your Story

Decide how to share your story. You might:

- Make a book of your story and pictures.

- Tell your story to a group of classmates. Show them the pictures as you talk.

- Put your story on your class website. Let others read it.

TIPS

- Make your treasure the center of your cluster map. Connect each part of your story to the treasure.

- Don't try to write about too many different events. Choose the best ones.

- Draw pictures that help tell the story.

Name_____

2. More from the Author

Goal: To read and discuss other books by Patricia Polacco.

Each member of your group chooses one book by Patricia Polacco and reads it. Then the group will meet and discuss the books. Before you meet, plan ahead what you'll say about your book. Think about:

- How is this book like *The Keeping Quilt?* How is it different?

- What did you like or dislike about the book?

TIPS

- Take turns speaking.
- Prepare notes on index cards. Use them during your discussion.
- Support your ideas with details from the book.

- Do you think others should read the book? Why or why not?

3. What Do You Think?

Goal: Evaluate the pictures in *The Keeping Quilt.*

Look at the pictures in *The Keeping Quilt* again. Take notes of your ideas. Think about:

- What do the pictures make you feel or think about?

- What do they add to the story?

- Do you like the pictures? Why or why not?

TIPS

- First, tell what you think about the pictures as a whole. Then tell about individual pictures.
- When you give your opinion, tell why and give examples.

Write a paragraph that gives your evaluation.

1. My Family Tradition

Goal: Write about someone who is important in your life.

Gather Details

Think of someone important to you. This person can be a relative, such as a favorite aunt, uncle, or grandparent, or just someone special to you. Describe what this person means to you, fond memories you have of him or her, and things you do together. Make notes to answer these questions:

- Why is this person important?
- What do you do together?
- Why do you enjoy being with him or her?

Write and Draw

Organize your writing. Tell why this person is special. Tell about special things you do. Tell how often you see him or her. Next, draw the two of you together.

TIPS

- Construct an outline to help organize your thoughts.
- Make notes of special times you've shared together.
- Use drawings to show what you do together.

Share Your Story

Decide how to share your writing. You could:

- Tell your classmates about this person. Show them the picture and explain what you do together.
- Tell how long you've known this person and different things you've learned from him or her.
- Make a copy of your writing. Put it in the class library.

Theme Paperback

2. *The Eyes of the Weaver*

Goal: To identify and discuss the main ideas in *The Eyes of the Weaver*.

Reread *The Eyes of the Weaver* and complete a Main Idea chart like the one on page 147 of the Practice Book. Meet with a group of classmates. Discuss the main ideas with them. Before you meet, plan what you'll say. Use your chart and take notes on these questions:

- What does the book's title mean?

- What does Cristina learn from Grandpa?

- What other traditions does Cristina learn?

- What is special about Grandpa's life?

- Should others read this book? Why or why not?

TIPS

- Support your ideas with details from the book.

- Take turns speaking.

- Prepare notes on index cards to use in your discussions.

3. How Does It Compare?

Goal: Compare and contrast two stories.

Choose another book or story about family traditions. Compare and contrast it to *Grandma's Records.* Use a comparison/contrast chart to take notes.

Then write two or three paragraphs that compare and contrast the books.

TIPS

- Organize your writing by categories.

- Give examples to show how things are alike and different.

Name_____

1. The Adinkra Cloth Says . . .

Goal: Create your own version of an adinkra cloth and then write about it.

Your Own Symbols

Reread pages 224–226 of *The Talking Cloth.* Then decide what you want to say in your cloth using symbols and colors. The symbols you choose should be meaningful to you. Think about

- what you like to do
- your goals
- your personality
- your family

Draw and Write

Plan your adinkra cloth. Draw each symbol in a pattern on a long piece of paper. Next, write about your adinkra. Make a chart that tells what each symbol and color means to you. In your chart, draw a picture of each symbol. Explain what each symbol and color means. Tell why they are important to you.

> **TIPS**
>
> - Plan what symbols and colors you will use in your drawing.
> - In your chart, write in complete sentences and give details to make your explanation clear.

Share Your Adinkra

Decide how you want to share your adinkra and your writing. You could:

- Display your adinkra. Point out the symbols and colors you used and tell what they mean.
- Place your chart and your adinkra on the bulletin board.

Name_____

2. Who Are the Ashanti?

Goal: Write a report about the Ashanti people.

Aunt Phoebe's adinkra cloth was made by the Ashanti people. Review *The Talking Cloth.* Read what it says about the Ashanti. Write down questions you have about the Ashanti people.

TIPS

- Specific details will make your report more interesting.

- Use a map or pictures to give information.

- Do research to find answers to your questions.

- Take notes as you read. Use index cards.

- Plan your report. Number the cards in the order you will tell the information. Use your cards as you write your report.

3. An Inch at a Time

Goal: Write about a time when you "grew an inch or two."

Aunt Phoebe says that Amber has grown "an inch or two, *inside.*" She means that Amber has learned something important. Write about a time when you grew "an inch or two inside." Be sure to tell

TIPS

- Use specific details to describe what happened.

- Draw pictures to help tell the story.

- what you learned

- where and when you learned it

- who helped you learn it

Name_____

1. Cultural Traditions

> **Goal:** Find out about a cultural tradition, craft, or art and present it to the class.

Gather Information

Choose a culture that interests you. Research that culture in an encyclopedia and other sources to find out about the traditions, crafts, and arts of that culture. Pick one that interests you. Take notes about

- how it started

- why it is made or celebrated

- who teaches or makes it

- any other important facts

TIPS

- Organize your main ideas before you begin. Number your note cards.

- Follow the cards as you plan your presentation.

Write It Down

Read through your notes. Decide what your main ideas are. Write each one at the top of an index card. Then write the supporting details for each main idea on each card.

Share Your Research

Use your notes to present your subject. Some ideas:

- If your subject is a craft or art, teach the class how to do or make it.

- Give an oral presentation to your class. Use visual aids such as posters, photographs, and hand-outs to help you.

- If your subject is a tradition, act it out for the class.

- Write a report and present it to the class.

Name_____

2. Who Are the Pueblo?

Goal: Write and give a short report about the Pueblo Indians.

The Tewa are one tribe of the Pueblo Indians. Learn more about the Pueblo. Answer these questions in your report, and think of others.

- Who are the Pueblo Indians?
- Where do they live?
- What are their traditions?

Write a one-page report. Include a map or a picture to help tell about the Pueblo.

TIPS

- Explain any unfamiliar words.
- Give at least two details for each main idea.
- Decide which information is best shown by a map or a picture.

3. Tell a Friend

Goal: Write a letter to a friend about seeing a Tewa dance.

Write a personal letter that tells about one of the Tewa dances as if you had seen it yourself. Include details from the selection and your own experience. Be sure to mention what you saw, heard, and felt.

TIPS

- Reread the descriptions of the Tewa dances in the story. Write useful details in a web.
- Use these details to write your letter and support your opinion.

Name_____

1. *Mousopolis Daily News*

Goal: Write a newspaper article on the invasion of Dogzilla.

Gather the News

The *Mousopolis Daily News* is the mouse newspaper. Imagine that you and your classmates are reporters for the paper. With a group of classmates, discuss Dogzilla's attack. Think about:

- What is Dogzilla?
- What damage did Dogzilla do?
- What did the mice do?

List topics that you want to write about. Divide them up. Every student will have a story to report. Use facts from *Dogzilla* to make up what the citizens of Mousopolis might think or say. Then write your article.

TIPS

- Come up with an exciting headline and an interesting opening sentence.
- Put all quotations in quotation marks. Tell who said the words each time.

Create the Newspaper

Work on your own, and make a newspaper page. Use a large piece of paper. Write a headline on your page. Decide what pictures you will include. Leave space on the page for them. Copy your story onto the page. Draw your pictures and captions in the blank spaces.

Read All About It!

Compile each of your pages into one paper. Invite your classmates to read your paper.

Name_____

2. Pupzilla

Goal: Write a sequel to *Dogzilla.*

What happens after the puppies appear in the volcano at the end of *Dogzilla?* Write a sequel to the story telling what happens next.

- Think about both real and fantastic events that could happen in your sequel.

- Plan your sequel using a fantasy and realism chart like the one on page 196 of the Practice Book.

- Use the puppies as your main characters.

TIPS

- Use details to describe the characters and setting.

- Tell about events in the order they happen.

- Use dialogue to bring the story alive.

- Write an ending that wraps up the story.

3. Volcano!

Goal: Write a report on a volcano that erupted in the United States.

Work with a partner to learn about Mount St. Helens. Research these questions:

- Where is Mount St. Helens? When has it erupted?

- How did the mountain and the land around it change when the volcano last erupted?

Write a report. Share what you learn with your class.

TIPS

- State the topic clearly in your opening sentence.

- Begin each paragraph with a main idea. Add supporting details.

- Include pictures, diagrams, and time lines.

Name_____

1. A Long Time Ago

Goal: Write a folktale set in a real place.

Plan Your Folktale

Look for ideas for the subject of your folktale in your community and in places around you. Think about

- natural settings like caves, streams, and mountains
- old statues, buildings, and tunnels

Imagine how these places might have been created. Think of stories that might have happened in these places. Write down a few ideas for some folktales.

Write and Draw

Use a story map to list the characters, describe the setting, and write the main plot events. Put them in the order they happen.

Now, write your folktale. Use your story map as your guide. Illustrate the most important scenes.

Share Your Folktale

Decide how you will share your folktale with your classmates. You might:

- Tell your folktale to your classmates. Show your pictures as you tell the story.

- Put your folktale on your class computer or school website.

- Include your story in a class collection of folktales.

TIPS

- Think up a difficult problem, then let your characters solve it.

- Present events in the order they happen.

Name_____

Theme Paperback

2. *Charlotte's Web*

Goal: Write and follow directions.

TIPS

- Number each step.
- Use signal words.
- Give precise directions.

Imagine that Charlotte's children don't know how to spell. With some classmates, choose a word to write for Wilbur. The word should have the same number of letters as there are members in your group. Write each letter on a slip of paper. Fold the papers. Each person takes a letter.

On your own, write step-by-step directions telling the spiders how to form your letter. When you finish, exchange directions with a classmate from your group. Follow the directions and write the letter. When everyone is done, put your letters together. Were your directions clear?

3. What a Day!

Goal: Write a journal entry for a soldier.

TIPS

- Use the words *I* and *we.*
- Include descriptions and explanations of important events.

Captain Minckion's soldiers have a very bad day. That night one of the soldiers writes a journal entry about the events of the day. Write the journal entry from his point of view. Think about

- the powerful army and its many victories
- the huge, sad boy and the people back in his town
- how the soldiers felt as they marched away

Name_____

1. A Dragon of Your Own

Goal: Write a story about raising your own dragon.

Plan Your Dragon Tale

Imagine that you find a dragon egg. Now you must figure out how to raise the dragon.

- Reread *Raising Dragons* and look at the pictures for more details and ideas.

- Use a story map to develop a beginning, middle, and end of your story.

Write and Draw

Write the story of raising your dragon. Tell the events in the order that they happen. Describe the setting using sensory details. Present a problem that gets solved. Include dialogue between your characters. Draw two or three pictures that would help tell the story.

Share Your Dragon Story

Share your story with others. Use one of these ideas:

TIPS

- Create a plot that has an interesting problem or situation.

- Stick to the main events in your story.

- Use details that help the reader see and hear what is happening.

- Make the pictures and story into a book. Put the pages together. Make a cover with a picture of you and your dragon. Staple it together. Let your classmates read it.

- Tell your story to a group of classmates. Pass around your pictures as you tell the tale.

2. When Dragons Grow Up

Goal: Draw conclusions about what to do after raising a dragon.

When and why should a dragon leave the farm? Look in the story for details to help you draw conclusions. Use a conclusions chart like the one on Practice Book page 231. Come up with at least three conclusions. Write your conclusions about raising dragons in a paragraph.

TIPS

- Take notes as you read the end of the story.

- Be sure to present all of your conclusions in your paragraph.

3. News at Six

Goal: Write a news report for a television station.

Imagine you are a reporter. Work with a partner to write a news report about Hank and the girl. Include an interview with questions and answers. Think about

- what it's like to live with a dragon

- what Hank thinks of the human world

- what their plans are

Share your news report with your class. One of you will be the reporter. The other will be the character who is interviewed. Act out the interview.

TIPS

- Be sure to answer the questions *Who? What? When? Where? Why?* and *How?*

- Present only the facts, except in the interview. The people being interviewed can give opinions.

Name _____

1. As Fritz Sees It

Goal: Write the story from Fritz's point of view.

Plan Your Story

Tell the story from Fritz's point of view. Explain what happened after he escaped from Alan.

Brainstorm ideas for your story. Take notes about these questions:

- Did Gasazi capture Fritz?

- Did they really turn Fritz into a duck? If not, where was Fritz and what was he doing?

Organize your story using a story map.

> ### TIPS
>
> - Imagine the problem that Fritz had to solve while Alan was looking for him.
>
> - Tell the events in the order that Fritz experienced them.

Write Your Story

Write Fritz's story. Some parts of the story won't change much. Other parts might be very different. Use your story map as a guide. Think about Fritz. What kind of dog is he? How would he tell the story? Add details that help the reader see and hear what is happening. Draw illustrations to help bring your story to life.

Share Your Story

Share your story with others. You could:

- Read your story to a group of classmates.

- Pass around your pictures while you tell your story to a group of classmates.

Name_____

2. Book Review

Goal: Write a book review.

When you review a book you tell about the characters, setting, and plot. You also tell what you like about it. Write a review of *The Garden of Abdul Gasazi.* Include answers to these questions:

- What do you like about the story?

- Did the story keep you interested? Why or why not?

- Do you think others should read the story? Why?

Share your review with a group. Discuss each other's opinions.

TIPS

- Make sure your opinions are separate from the facts of the story.

- Give details from the story to support your opinions.

3. Gardens Galore!

Goal: Write about gardens.

There are many kinds of gardens. Write about two or three different kinds of gardens. Think about:

- Why are there different kinds of gardens?

- What is the purpose of each kind of garden?

- Where can you find each of these kinds of gardens?

Add your own questions. Research the questions. Write a report. Draw pictures to help explain the different kinds of gardens.

TIPS

- Think about gardens you have visited or seen. How were they alike and different?

- Look for answers to your questions in different sources.

Name_____

1. Animal Habitat Mural

Goal: Create and present a mural that shows animals in their habitats.

Gather Information

Working in a small group, brainstorm a list of animals. Have each member of your group look up an animal in an encyclopedia or books on animals. Find out about your animal's habitat. Answer these questions:

TIPS

- Be sure to make a sketch of your panel before you draw.
- Present your mural in the order it is drawn.

- What does the habitat look like?

- What is the animal's home?

- What does the animal eat?

Make notes about your animal and its habitat on index cards.

Draw Your Mural

Plan out your mural panel.

- Draw a sketch of what you want to include in your panel.

- Use the sketches to decide the order of your panels.

- Draw and color your panel on a large sheet of butcher paper.

- Label the animals and plants in your habitat.

Present Your Mural

Hang your mural on the board with tape and present it to the class. Each member of the group should present his or her panel.

Name_____

2. Animals Around Us

Goal: Write a description of a wild animal that you see every day.

What wild animals do you see all the time? Choose one kind of animal and write a description of it. Tell what facts you know about it. Use an encyclopedia to learn more about it. Give your opinion of it. Be sure to

- tell where you see the animal

- describe what it looks like

- tell what you know about how it lives

TIPS

- Select an animal that you find interesting.

- Be specific. Tell what the animal looks and sounds like. Describe its behavior.

3. Dear Halla

Goal: Write a letter to Halla. Tell her about something important you do with your friends every year.

Halla looks forward to the nights of the pufflings. She and her friends stay up late to help the young birds. Write a letter to Halla and tell her about something that you do with your friends. Tell her what you do, when you do it, why you do it, and what you like about it.

TIPS

- List details about your activity. Number them in the order you want to tell about them.

- Write a friendly letter. Use the words *I* and *we.*

Name_____

1. Two Kinds of Seals

Goal: Compare and contrast two kinds of seals.

Gather Information

Did you know there are many kinds of seals? Do research and learn about some of these seals. Pick two kinds of seals to compare and contrast. Think about

- what they look like
- where they live
- how they live

Take Notes

Take notes as you read. Write each main idea at the top of an index card. Write details that tell more about each main idea on each card.

TIPS

- Include only facts about your topic.
- Use illustrations to show the different kinds of seals. Use maps to show where they live.

Compare and Contrast

Use a Venn diagram.

- Label each circle with the names of the two kinds of seals.
- Fill in the center circle with phrases that tell how the seals are alike. Fill in each side circle with phrases that tell how the seals are different.
- Give an oral report to a group of classmates to tell about the seals you picked. Use illustrations and a map to give more information.

Name _____

2. Surfing

Goal: Write and illustrate a report on surfing.

What do you know about surfing? Think about these questions:

- How and where do people surf?
- What skills are needed for surfing?

Research surfing in an encyclopedia. Then organize your information and write a paragraph. Use pictures to help tell about surfing. Write captions for each picture. Put your work on the classroom bulletin board.

TIPS

- Be sure to include a clear topic sentence.
- Think about someone who knows nothing about surfing. What details would he or she need to know to understand it?

Theme Paperback

3. *In Good Hands*

Goal: Have a discussion about how people can help animals and plants.

Hannah works hard at the raptor center to save birds. Do you think it is important to save an orphaned owl? Look for information in *In Good Hands* and in other books as well. Think about why it might be important to help things in nature. Then get together with three classmates. Talk about and give reasons for your opinion. Discuss some ways people can help animals and plants.

TIPS

- Think about what you've learned from reading about this topic.
- Listen carefully to your classmates' opinions.

Name _____

1. Nowhere to Go

Goal: Decide what people can do to help animals who are losing their habitats.

TIPS

- Express your opinion clearly.
- Give reasons for your solution.
- Support your reasons with facts.

Gather Information

Animals are losing their homes. What can people do to help? Use books, magazines, and encyclopedias to do research. Look for facts about

- how animal habitats are changing
- what kinds of animals are losing their homes
- what people are doing to help

Think About the Problem

Make a problem-solving chart like the one below. List as many possible solutions as you can. List the pros and cons of each solution. Select the best idea.

Problem: How to help animals who are losing their habitats.		
Solutions: 1. 2. 3.	Pros:	Cons:
Which solution is best and why?		

Share Your Information

Share what you've learned. You might write an opinion essay to read to the class, or make a pamphlet that states the problem and solution to hang on a classroom bulletin board.

Name_____

2. In My Opinion . . .

Goal: Read about a problem and make a judgment about the solution.

TIPS

- State your opinion in the opening.
- Give reasons and facts to support your opinion.
- Sum up your reasons and opinion in your closing.

Read a magazine article or a book about an animal habitat or the environment. Make sure it states a problem and offers a solution. Think about the opinions, reasons, and facts given. Make a decision chart similar to the one on Practice Book page 39 to help you weigh the ideas. Decide if you think the solution is the best one. Then write an essay stating whether you agree or disagree, and why. If you disagree, tell what you think should be done.

3. *Two Days In May*

Goal: Write the story from the point of view of one of the deer.

Imagine what it might have been like for the deer in *Two Days in May.* Think about these points:

- The deer were hungry and far from home.
- They were in a strange place filled with humans, buildings, and cars.

Now rewrite the story. Tell it from the point of view of one of the deer.

TIPS

- Write a beginning that makes your audience curious.
- Include details that tell what the deer saw, heard, and felt.

Name_____

1. A Story About Squanto

Goal: Write historical fiction that tells about an important visitor to the Pilgrims' settlement.

Gather Information

Use an encyclopedia or another reference source to learn more about Squanto. Take notes.

Write Your Story

Choose one time in Squanto's life to tell about. Build your story around that event. Use a story map to organize your ideas.

- Describe the setting.

- Develop your plot. Begin with a real problem that Squanto faced. Add events that tell how he tried to solve the problem.

- Add realistic details. Tell what the characters think and feel.

Put it together and write your story.

Share Your Historical Fiction

Decide how you want to share your story. You might:

- Create an illustrated book.

- Read or tell your story aloud to a group of classmates.

- Post your story on the classroom computer.

TIPS

- Stick to the facts from your research.

- Use real people from that time as characters, if possible.

2. Our First Conversation

Goal: Write a dialogue between a Pilgrim and an Indian.

In *Across the Wide Dark Sea,* you read that in March, an Indian walked into the Pilgrims' settlement and said, "Welcome." What do you think the Pilgrims said in response? What do you imagine their first conversation was like? Use details from the story and what you know to make inferences about what they might have talked about. Write dialogue. Then read it aloud with a partner.

TIPS

- Think about what the Pilgrims had already experienced.

- Think about why the Indian might have visited the Pilgrims.

3. Journey in Time

Goal: Write a story about a journey back to the time of the Pilgrims.

You can't actually go back in time. But you can travel in your mind and visit other times and places.

Take a trip in your mind to the time of the *Mayflower.* Write about your journey and what you find in the Pilgrims' new home. Reread pages 170–177 of *Across the Wide Dark Sea.* Write about your visit.

TIPS

- Think about what the Pilgrims might have heard and seen.

- Take notes as you read.

Name_____

1. Travel Guide

Goal: Write a travel guide for Korea.

Gather Information

Look back at *Yunmi and Halmoni's Trip.* Make a list of the places they visit. Look in an encyclopedia, Atlas, or on the Internet to find more places you would like to see. Use a K-W-L chart to take notes as you read. Think about

- cities

- museums, monuments, and other buildings

- mountains, rivers, and other natural places

Write Your Travel Guide

Pick the most interesting places to include in your travel guide. Don't try to include everything. How will you organize your writing? As you write, use the following:

- headings and subheadings

- pictures and maps

- captions

Share Your Travel Guide

Decide how to publish your travel guide. You could:

- Make a brochure. Fold sheets of paper in half like a book. Put your information on the inside. Draw a picture and title for the cover.

- Create a bulletin board display.

- Make a poster. Hang it on the wall.

TIPS

- Think about your audience. Be sure to give them enough information.

- Give specific details.

2. Will You Visit?

Goal: Write a story about Yunmi and her cousins.

- Think about Yunmi's friendship with her cousins.

- Think about what Halmoni tells Yunmi at the end.

At the end of the story, Yunmi wants to invite her cousins, Sunhi and Jinhi, to visit her in New York. Think about these questions:

- What will they say?

- What will it be like for Yunmi to say goodbye before she leaves?

Predict the outcome using clues from the story. Write a story that tells what happens after the end of the selection.

3. *Balto and the Great Race*

Theme Paperback

Goal: Compare and contrast *Balto and the Great Race* with another animal story.

- Use a Venn diagram or comparison/ contrast chart to organize your ideas.

- Give examples to support your opinions.

- Give details when you make comparisons.

How does *Balto and the Great Race* compare to another book about animals that you have read? Organize your ideas and opinions. Then write a comparison of the two books. For each book think about these questions:

- Who is telling the story?

- Is it a true story or fiction?

- What makes the story interesting?

Name _____

1. The Arctic and Antarctica

Goal: Compare and contrast the Arctic with Antarctica.

TIPS

- Focus on *comparing* and *contrasting.*
- Organize your information so it is easy to read. Use headings, titles, captions, and labels.

Find the Facts

Many people get Antarctica confused with the Arctic.

- Use a Venn diagram. Label one circle *Antarctica,* the other *Arctic,* and the overlapping area *Both*.

- Fill in facts that you already know about Antarctica from reading *Trapped by the Ice!*

- Use an encyclopedia to find facts about the Arctic. What lives there? What are the summer and winter temperatures?

- Fill in any facts that apply to both regions.

Compare the Facts

Read the information in your diagram. What else would you like to find out? Use an encyclopedia to find other information for both the Arctic and Antarctica, such as any explorers who have visited the regions.

Share What You Know

Decide how to present your information. You could:

- Write a report.

- Make a "picture essay." Draw several pictures and write captions to show what you have learned.

- Give an oral presentation to the class.

2. What's in a Name?

Goal: Write an opinion paragraph about the name of Shackleton's ship.

Was *Endurance* a good name for Shackleton's ship? Write an opinion paragraph to answer this question. Be sure to

- explain the meaning of the word *endurance*

- give your opinion and reasons for your opinion

- include details from the story that explain your reasons

TIPS

- Include a definition of the word *endurance* in your paragraph.

- Think about story events, characters, and actions.

3. A Crew Member's Letter

Goal: Write a personal letter as if you were a crew member on *Endurance*.

The crew of *Endurance* depended on Shackleton's leadership to survive. Write a personal letter that describes Shackleton. Think about Shackleton's

- actions

- decisions

- judgment

- concern for the crew

TIPS

- First brainstorm a list of ideas about Shackleton's character. Then find story details to support your ideas.

- Use the five parts of a letter: heading, greeting, body, closing, and signature.

1. Smart Comic Strip Solutions

Goal: Create a comic strip that shows a smart solution to an everyday problem.

Choose a Problem and Plan a Solution

- Work with a partner. Brainstorm a list of everyday problems. Choose a problem to solve.

- Figure out an unusual, clever solution. Don't look for easy solutions. Use the picture on page 296 to get you started.

- List the steps in your solution. It should have at least five steps. Make a cause-effect chart. Draw or write the steps in each box. Add as many boxes as you need.

Create Your Comic Strip

Now draw your comic strip solution. Be sure to

- show all the steps

- make the problem and solution clear in your pictures

- use labels, arrows, letters, or numbers to help the reader understand what happens

- at the bottom of your comic strip write explanations

TIPS

- Invent a complicated solution to an easy problem.

- Show how each step is connected.

Share Your Comic Strip

Choose one of the following ways to share your comic strip:

- Make a poster. Show all the steps in a single picture.

- Make a long comic strip. Show the steps in a row of boxes.

- Make a comic book. Show one step on each page.

Name_____

2. Problems, Problems, Problems

Goal: Write your opinion of what the characters did to solve a problem.

Read another book, such as *Three Days on a River in a Red Canoe* or *How the Stars Fell into the Sky.* Choose an important problem the characters faced. Fill in a problem-solution chart like the one on page 168 of the Practice Book to help you. Then write a short opinion essay. Tell whether you

TIPS

- Think of your own solutions.
- Look at the problem from the characters' point of view.

think the characters make the right decision. Explain why. If you disagree with their solution, tell why and provide another one.

3. In My Opinion

Goal: Write a pretend letter to Pepita, giving a solution to her problem from the point of view of another character in the story.

TIPS

- Look for clues about what the character thinks Pepita should or shouldn't do.
- What would that character say to Pepita? How would he or she say it?

- Pick a character from the story that isn't Pepita.

- Review *Pepita Talks Twice.* Look for clues in the story that tell how the character would solve Pepita's problem.

- Write a letter from that character to Pepita, suggesting a solution and explaining why it makes sense.

Grade 3 Theme 6: Smart Solutions

Challenge Master **CH 6–2**

Copyright © Houghton Mifflin Company. All rights reserved.

1. It Was So Funny . . .

> **Goal:** Write a story about a funny personal experience.

Plan Your Funny Story

Think of a time when you saw or experienced something really funny. Then gather details. Take notes as you think about

- what happened
- where and when it happened
- who was there

Then make a story map. Fill in the details telling what you saw, heard, and felt.

> **TIPS**
>
> - Tell your story from your point of view.
> - Use specific details.
> - Use exaggeration to add humor.

Write Your Story

Your story should have a beginning, a middle, and an end. When you write

- introduce your characters at the beginning of the story
- tell events in the order they happened
- write an ending that wraps up the story
- include dialogue to define the characters and move the action along
- include all the humorous elements in your plot

Share Your Story

Share your story with your classmates. Use one of these ideas.

- Post your story on your class computer or school website.
- Make your story into a book by adding drawings.
- Practice telling your story aloud. Then tell it to the class.

Name_____

2. Grandma Tiny Speaks

Goal: Write Grandma Tiny's version of *Poppa's New Pants.*

Learn more about Grandma Tiny by making inferences and drawing conclusions. Reread the story. Look carefully at what she says and does. Now tell the story from her point of view. Write the story as though Grandma Tiny were telling it to a friend.

TIPS

- Make a character web of Grandma Tiny.

- Look at the pictures. What do they tell you about Grandma Tiny?

- Think about her feelings toward George and Poppa.

Theme Paperback

3. *Stealing Home*

Goal: Write a short essay comparing two authors' viewpoints.

You've read *Poppa's New Pants* and *Stealing Home.* Both end with smart solutions. How do these two authors feel about dealing with problems? Draw conclusions. Look at

- how the author describes characters and events

- what their characters do when they face problems

- what the authors say about unexpected problems and solutions

Write a short essay comparing the two authors' viewpoints.

TIPS

- Ask the same questions of each story.

- Support your opinion with examples and details from the stories.

- Include a conclusion that summarizes the important points.

Name_____

1. Another Sunday

Goal: Write a story about another Sunday when the Quimbys meet the old man again.

Plan Your Story

Write a story about another time the Quimbys meet the old man. Think about what might happen.

- Where might the Quimbys meet the old man again?

- What do you think they would say or ask each other?

- How would they feel?

Come up with several possible answers to each question. Based on the story, which of your answers are most possible?

TIPS

- Use dialogue.
- Include details that show what your characters see, hear, and feel.
- Make sure your characters act and talk the way they did in the original story.

Write Your Story

Before you begin writing, complete a story map. Use the map to guide you as you write. Describe the setting and characters. Decide on a problem and how the characters will solve it. Decide on the order of the major events in your story. Now write your story.

Share Your Story

Decide how you want to share your story. You could:

- Read your story aloud to a group of classmates.

- Publish your story on your class computer or website.

- Make a collection of classroom stories. Put all your stories together. Make a cover.

2. Beverly Cleary's Books

Goal: Make generalizations about other Beverly Cleary books.

Begin by choosing another book by Beverly Cleary. Read it on your own. Take notes as you read. Think about what it has in common with *Ramona Quimby, Age 8.* Think about setting, characters, problems, and solutions.

Now meet with a group of classmates. Take turns telling about the book you have read and making generalizations about books by Beverly Cleary. Work together as a group to fill out a generalizations chart about her books.

TIPS

• Think about what elements are in both books.

• Think about the problems the characters face. How are they the same?

3. Book Review

Goal: Write a book review.

Did you like *Ramona Quimby, Age 8?* Write a book review and give your opinion. Think about:

• What did you think of the characters?

• Did the plot keep you interested? Why?

• What did you think of the pictures?

• Do you think other students would enjoy the book? Why or why not?

TIPS

• Make a list of what you did and didn't like about the book.

• Give reasons and details from the book to support your opinions.

Web

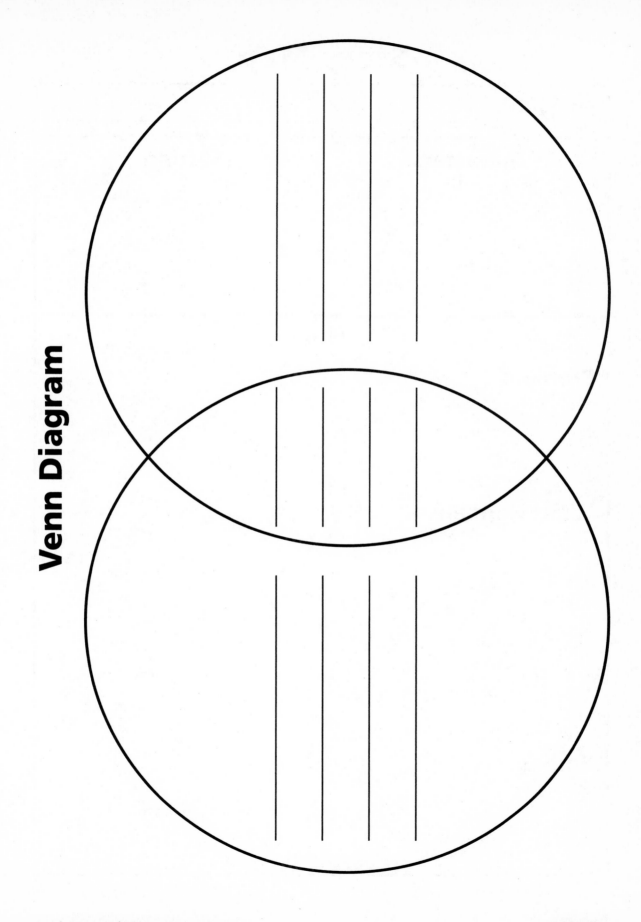

Venn Diagram

Grade 3 Graphic Organizer Master 2

CH GO–2

Story Map

Title: _____

Characters	Setting

Plot

Problem

What Happens

Ending

K-W-L Chart

What I **K**now	What I **W**ant to Learn	What I **L**earned

Main Idea Chart

Topic:_____

Pages_____   **Main Idea:**_____

_____

Details:

1. _____

2. _____

Pages_____   **Main Idea:**_____

_____

Details:

1. _____

2. _____

Pages_____   **Main Idea:**_____

_____

Details:

1. _____

2. _____

Problem/Solution Chart

Problem: _____

Possible Solutions	Pros (+) and Cons (—)
1. _____ _____ _____ _____	(+) _____ _____ (–) _____ _____
2. _____ _____ _____ _____	(+) _____ _____ (–) _____ _____
3. _____ _____ _____ _____	(+) _____ _____ (–) _____ _____
4. _____ _____ _____ _____	(+) _____ _____ (–) _____ _____

Compare and Contrast Chart

Topic 1: _____	Topic 2: _____

Conclusions Chart

Story Details		Story Details		Conclusion
page _____ _____ _____ _____	**+**	page _____ _____ _____ _____	**=**	_____ _____ _____ _____
page _____ _____ _____ _____	**+**	page _____ _____ _____ _____	**=**	_____ _____ _____ _____
page _____ _____ _____ _____	**+**	page _____ _____ _____ _____	**=**	_____ _____ _____ _____
page _____ _____ _____ _____	**+**	page _____ _____ _____ _____	**=**	_____ _____ _____ _____

Generalizations Chart

In general, what statement can you make about

_____ **?**

_____

_____